This book will
who put their t

This is one of the most insightful, accessible, engaging, and practical works I have read on Revelation 2 and 3. *Revive* powerfully blends fresh historical background, contemporary illustrations, convicting challenges, and pragmatic applications to move the reader past inspiration to obedience.

—**Larry J. Walkemeyer**, director of spiritual formation for Exponential

Revive is a wonderful small-group or personal discipleship resource to help those of us who have been following Christ for years rekindle the passion and commitment that fueled us when we first received the grace of salvation.

—**Colleen R. Derr**, president of Wesley Seminary

[This book] is more than just education—the call of the Holy Spirit leaps off every page. I am convinced that people and groups who read, study, and live out this book will become pockets of awakenings throughout the globe.

—**Jo Anne Lyon**, general superintendent emerita of the Wesleyan Church

This book will awaken you to what the Spirit is doing in the church today and revive your faith.

—**Winfield Bevins**, director of church planting at Asbury Seminary and author of *Marks of a Movement*

The spiritual lessons Love draws from the letters are practical and encouraging. You will enjoy the timeless truths packed in these short and gripping words written to fellow Christians millennia ago, whose lives and struggles were not so different from our own.

—**David Wright**, president of
Indiana Wesleyan University

Ed Love has a knack for pulling back the curtain on what was really going on in the original contexts of the Bible. This [book] helps you understand the world of the Word better, and also live in your world more faithfully.

—**David Drury**, author of
more than a dozen books

Ed Love handles the book of Revelation with rich scholarship and a generous orthodoxy that will help the entire body of Christ. *Revive* is a very practical, grounded, and challenging read for everyday disciples. I was educated, inspired, and challenged by this book.

—**Rob Wegner**, Kansas City Underground Catalyst
and author of *Starfish and the Spirit*

Ed Love's humor, heart-warming stories, and deep truths have me refocusing on Jesus and breathing new life into my soul.

—**Ralph Moore**, church multiplier and
author of *Making Disciples*.

REVIVE

REVIVE

HOW THE SEVEN LETTERS OF REVELATION CAN

AWAKEN YOUR SOUL

 Seedbed

Scripture quotations, unless otherwise indicated, are taken from the Holy Bible,
New International Version®, NIV®. Copyright © 1973, 1978, 1984, 2011 by
Biblica, Inc.™ Used by permission of Zondervan. All rights reserved worldwide.
www.zondervan.com The "NIV" and "New International Version" are trademarks
registered in the United States Patent and Trademark Office by Biblica, Inc.™

Scripture quotations marked NLT are taken from the Holy Bible, New Living Translation,
copyright ©1996, 2004, 2015 by Tyndale House Foundation. Used by permission of
Tyndale House Publishers, Carol Stream, Illinois 60188. All rights reserved.

Scripture quotations marked The Message are taken from THE MESSAGE,
copyright © 1993, 2002, 2018 by Eugene H. Peterson. Used by permission of
NavPress, represented by Tyndale House Publishers. All rights reserved.

Printed in the United States of America

Cover design by Kevin Tucker at Collide Creative
Page design by PerfecType, Nashville, Tennessee

Love, Ed (Pastor)
  Revive : how the seven letters of Revelation can awaken your soul / Ed Love. –
Franklin, Tennessee : Seedbed Publishing, ©2022.

        pages ; cm.

        Includes bibliographical references.
        ISBN: 9781628249309 (paperback)
        ISBN: 9781628249316 (mobi)
        ISBN: 9781628249323 (epub)
        ISBN: 9781628249330 (pdf)
        OCLC: 1291321431

        1. Bible. Revelation, II-III--Criticism, interpretation, etc.
        2. Seven churches. 3. Spiritual life--Christianity.   I. Title.

BS2825.52.L68 2022   228.06   2022930387

 Seedbed

SEEDBED PUBLISHING
Franklin, Tennessee
seedbed.com

This book is for anyone who wonders if it is possible to re-experience the vibrant passion they once had for Jesus, the Scriptures, and the mission of the church.

If you are ready to be reawakened, revived, and reinvigorated with real faith, then these pages are for you.

"Therefore let all Israel be assured of this: God has made this Jesus, whom you crucified, both Lord and Messiah."

When the people heard this, they were cut to the heart and said to Peter and the other apostles, "Brothers, what shall we do?"

—Acts 2:36–37

Contents

Introduction: The Missing Ingredient   1

1 | Ephesus—First and Foremost   7

2 | Smyrna—Faithful and Fearless   25

3 | Pergamum—Loyal and Listening   43

4 | Thyatira—Improving and Intentional   59

5 | Sardis—Alive and Alarmed   75

6 | Philadelphia—Persevering and Passionate   95

7 | Laodicea—Rich and Radical   107

Conclusion: Consumed and Concerned   121

Notes   131

Introduction

The Missing Ingredient

"Wake up, sleeper, rise from the dead, and Christ will shine on you."

Be very careful, then, how you live—not as unwise but as wise, making the most of every opportunity, because the days are evil.

—Ephesians 5:14b–16

J ennah! What happened to our cookies?"

"I don't know, Dad. Did we leave something out?"

"Ah shoot, I know what we forgot! We forgot the baking soda!"

• • •

Ever since a child, I have enjoyed baking chocolate chip cookies. Over the years, I have perfected a recipe, which in my tribe is respectfully known as The Love Batch.

Throughout my lifetime, I have baked thousands of cookies, and my recipe is entrenched in my memory bank. However, on this particular day, my daughter and I were rushing through the baking process and we forgot something—something very important. As soon as the cookies came out of the oven, I noticed they didn't look fabulous and fluffy—they were flat, floppy, and not very enticing to eat.

Similar to the distractions during my baking episode, there are a lot of things in life which sidetrack us from our relationship with God. Sometimes we can become so busy and consumed with life that we forget the one ingredient which makes all the difference.

Life is ridiculously rushed. Work, school, kids, relationships, family, recreation, events, groups, and hobbies all are competing for our time, talent, and treasure. Truth be told, there are far more circumstances pulling us away from Jesus than pushing us closer to him.

When it comes to our relationship with God, most of us can relate to the feeling of being flat, floppy, and distant from God. In our core, we desire to be alive in Christ, but sometimes we settle for life in Groggyville.

Most of us know what it's like to be in that sleepy and distant condition. We know we are missing the snap, crackle, and pop of God's best, but we can't seem to remain in a consistent state of revival. If we are honest, sometimes our most consistent trait is being inconsistent.

How do we avoid letting our commitment to following Jesus wane? Is there a faith-perspective that will continue to keep us connected and growing in Christ? Did God give us a picture of what this type of life could look like?

• • •

Throughout the Scriptures, God paints portrait after portrait of what life with him can look like if we choose to be all in—sold out to him and his mission in the world.

One of my favorite kaleidoscopic portraits is found in the opening section of the book of Revelation. In chapters 2 and 3, the author, John, presents us with seven short letters, written to seven churches, with seven different life-changing messages. Bear in mind, Jesus' seven different messages were originally written to specific churches, but like all Scripture, these ancient messages are incredibly relevant for everyone in every age.

Within this book, my goal is to unpack each letter and message in a fresh way, so you can absorb and apply John's original intent. In the end, I hope you will see the difference between chasing an unattainable happy life and pursuing a holy life filled with abundant joy. To be sure, Jesus was far more concerned about our holiness than our happiness. However, if you understand holiness properly, you will see how holy living will lead to fulfillment in this life. The order is important.

As we journey through these power-packed letters, we will begin by exploring the historical, cultural, and contextual backdrop of each of the churches John wrote. After we discover John's original intent, then we will apply the messages to our lives and, hopefully, God's Spirit will penetrate our hearts and revive us again.

• • •

The year of 2020 will forever be engrained in our minds. For most of the world, 2020 will be remembered by quarantines, financial pressure, schedule changes, and masks. We will never forget the masks!

The worldwide pandemic certainly has been and continues to be a challenge, and has undoubtedly changed our lives in many ways. However, it was not all bad. One event had us looking to the stars again.

On May 30, 2020, Elon Musk's private space company, SpaceX, launched NASA astronauts Bob Behnken and Doug Hurley into outer space. Beyond the achievement for SpaceX, the launch represented the first time NASA has sent its own astronauts since the end of the space shuttle program nearly a decade before.

The uniquely designed SpaceX capsule set its sights on the International Space Station, with the goal to make these sorts of exploratory missions more regular. Future missions will include space tourism for privately paying people to sightsee the wonders of the galaxy. After the historic launch, NASA deputy administrator Jim Morhard stated: "We're at the dawn of a new age and we're really leading the beginning of a space revolution."[1]

Oftentimes life feels like an immobilized space program. The lights are off, the engine is cool, and the rocket fuel is stagnant. Yet we know God's not done. God's mission of hope must prevail. God is still longing for innovative souls to rise up, turn on the lights, and fire up the rocket boosters!

Staying lit and remaining alive in Christ certainly is challenging, but the world is desperate and wondering if there are any SpaceX–like Christians. Is there anybody who has joy even when the world is falling apart? Is there anybody who can advance the mission of God when the world is shutting down? Is there anybody that can faithfully endure opposition and persecution? Is there anybody who won't bow down to the idols of our modern culture? Is there anybody who will allow Jesus to be their guiding authority in life? Anybody?

It seems as if God's people are constantly craving and calling for revival in the land. This impulse isn't a bad thing, but it's important to recognize that revival cannot be orchestrated or controlled. Revival outbreak always starts and spreads with one soul filled with fiery faith.

I believe we're at the dawn of a new age and a revolutionary revival is on the way. There are many SpaceX–like Christians scattered throughout the world, and more and more will be raised up within the emerging generations.

Maybe you will be one. Let's go on a journey to discover how to die to our selfish impulses and resurrect with a genuine experience of personal revival that will stand the test of time!

1 | **Ephesus**

First and Foremost

> *We have suffered from the preaching of cheap grace. Grace is free, but it is not cheap. People will take anything that is free, but they are not interested in discipleship. They will take Christ as Savior but not as Lord.*
>
> —Vance Havner

In the year 2000, I moved from southern Missouri to northern Michigan, with the purpose of leading a student ministry in a well-respected church. As I entered into the northern realm, I quickly picked up on many cultural differences from the South to the North. Northerners were constantly making fun of my Southern drawl and how I said certain words like *wersh* instead of *wash*. Yes, that's right, I wersh my cloths!

One of the social observations I discovered was how the northern region had two romantic holidays. Of course, there is the universally accepted Valentine's Day, but somewhere along the way someone decided the Great Lakes region needed another day in early October to get romantic. This additional romantic holiday is known as Sweetest Day.

When I first learned about this new Hallmark holiday, my cynical mind assumed it was created so flower businesses and candy shops could increase their revenue. Initially, I was opposed and outraged with the creation of another, culturally enforced, romantic holiday.

However, I quickly noticed something about my relationship with my wife. Without certain romantic checkpoints along the way, it is really easy to forget about her romantic needs. If my wife and I were to be honest, there have been several points within our relationship when we both could describe how our relationship "doesn't feel like it used to."

As humans, we are prone to drifting and settling for second best. Most of us, at some point in our love-filled relationships, will become complacent and take our loved one for granted.

We tend to do the same with God too.

The drifting and settling factors are some of the first things we need to be aware of in order to live fully alive as a follower of Jesus. This is the primary subject being addressed within the first letter found in the book of Revelation.

As you read this letter, and the other letters in the following chapters, take your time and pay extra attention to the metaphors and images John utilizes. We will unpack them in further detail. Here is John's letter to the church in Ephesus, transmitted through the voice of Jesus:

"Write this letter to the angel of the church in Ephesus. This is the message from the one who holds the seven stars in his right hand, the one who walks among the seven gold lampstands:

"I know all the things you do. I have seen your hard work and your patient endurance. I know you don't tolerate evil people. You have examined the claims of those who say they are apostles but are not. You have discovered they are liars. You have patiently suffered for me without quitting.

"But I have this complaint against you. You don't love me or each other as you did at *first*! Look how far you have fallen! Turn back to me and do the works you did at *first*. If you don't repent, I will come and remove your lampstand from its place among the churches. But this is in your favor: You hate the evil deeds of the Nicolaitans, just as I do.

"Anyone with ears to hear must listen to the Spirit and understand what he is saying to the churches. To everyone who is victorious I will give fruit from the tree of life in the paradise of God." (Rev. 2:1–7 NLT, emphasis added)

Ephesus 101

When we know something of the history of Ephesus and understand the cultural dynamics involved, it is easy to see why it comes first in the list of the seven churches, and why Jesus said, "Turn back to me and do the works you did at first" (Rev. 2:5 NLT). Plus, if the mail carrier was coming from the Roman exilic island of Patmos, where John was writing from, Ephesus would have been the natural first stop.[1]

Within the first century, Pergamum was the capital of the province of Asia, but Ephesus was by far the greatest city in the region. Despite competition with both, Ephesus had proved more powerful than Pergamum politically and more favored by the Roman government than Smyrna.[2]

Since Ephesus was considered the gateway to Asia, a Roman writer once called Ephesus the *Lumen Asiae*, the Light of Asia.[3] By the time John wrote his letter, the city had a growing population of more than 250,000. It was home to one of the major harbors in the region and most of the significant highways went through Ephesus on the way to Rome. In addition, Ephesus was the home of the most famous annual games in Asia and people came from all over the region to engage in the diverse festivities.[4] Because of its location, Ephesus was one of the wealthiest and greatest cities in all of Asia.

Ephesus was also the center for the worship of Artemis, otherwise known as Diana of the Ephesians. The Temple of Artemis is considered one of the Seven Wonders of the Ancient World. It was 425 feet long and 220 feet wide. It had 120 columns, each reaching 60 feet high. The image of Artemis was one of the most consecrated images in the ancient world.

Even more, Ephesus had many famous temples dedicated to the godhead of the Roman emperors such as Claudius, Nero, and Domitian—all beast-like persecutors of the early Christians. People would come from far away to worship the deity of Caesar within the Ephesian temples.[5]

The portrait of an evil world ruler demanding worship (Rev. 13:12–15) would certainly be relevant to Christians in Ephesus, who found themselves surrounded by symbols of civil religion. Caesar Augustus had allowed officials in Ephesus to build two temples in his honor, and Caesar Domitian had named Ephesus "guardian" of the imperial cult, making it the foremost center of the imperial cult in Roman Asia.[6] As you can imagine, this dynamic created a lot of cultural tensions for the Ephesian Christ-followers.

One might assume Christianity struggled to grow in such a hostile environment, but quite the opposite occurred. Nowhere in the first century did the Word of God find better soil and bear more fruit than in Ephesus.

The church in Ephesus experienced a great start, but as the church soon discovered, the goal of any church is not merely having a great start, but to have a lasting impact.

The message to Ephesian believers seems to present a picture of a faithful church. Even though they were situated in the center of pagan and Caesar worship, they were still willing to live as citizens of the newly founded kingdom of God, where Jesus is King of kings and Lord of lords.

In the revelatory letter, Jesus positively noted how his disciples in Ephesus were working hard, enduring many trials, and not tolerating wickedness. Jesus also mentioned they had resisted many false teachers, especially the Nicolaitans. Historians do not know much about the Nicolaitans, but we do know Jesus did not like their beliefs and practices.

Even though the church in Ephesus had a proper theological foundation, there was one very important area missing within the church: the area of love—both the love for God and the love of others.[7]

Apparently, the Christ-followers in Ephesus had lost the core value which first made them into an influential church community.

On the Ball

In most competitive sports, there are two sides to each team: the offense and defense. Both sides are necessary if a team desires to win the game. The offensive side scores the points, and the defensive side protects the scoreboard from further damage.

Likewise, in the church, there is a need for a defensive and offensive team. God's people need to protect the mission from the opposition, and they need to advance God's mission of love down the field.

In the case of the Ephesian church, they had dropped the ball when it came to the offensive movement of love. Instead, the church had begun to adopt a defensive posture, focusing solely on protecting their people from theological error.

Jesus applauded the Ephesian church for not supporting the Nicolaitans. Protecting the church from bad doctrine, faulty beliefs, and immorality is certainly necessary, but Jesus knew if the church in Ephesus did not get on the ball and start playing offense, then they might as well throw in the towel.

Like a good coach, Jesus encouraged his Ephesian team to get back on the playing field, return to the game of eternal life, and put his love first once again.

Reprioritizing

The first time for anything is like an engraving on the soul. I can still remember many of my firsts—my first bicycle, Nintendo, remote-controlled car, girlfriend, kiss, motorcycle, car, house, youth ministry, church plant, and church-planting network.

I can also remember when I first encountered Jesus in a very real way. I was on a spelunking trip with my church's youth ministry. On one particular evening, the leaders started singing worship songs around the campfire. One of the songs God used to touch my heart was Rich Mullins's, "Our God Is an Awesome God." This spontaneous worship session was the first time I truly encountered God, and this moment is forever engraved on my soul. Something awakened in me and I knew God was awesome.

Most Christ-followers can name the time and place where they first encountered the powerful presence of Jesus. They can recall the atmosphere, the message, and the entire enrapturing experience.

In the letter to the church of Ephesus, we see Jesus calling his disciples back to their first experience with him and with one another. We can imagine the feeling they had at their first encounter with meeting a need, adding value to a lost soul, or teaching the truth of God's Word. Yet, over time, the newness factor wore off and other things began taking priority over the ways of Jesus.

One of the disciplines in life my wife and I try to put into practice is when we first see each other, after a long day of work, we erupt with joy and act like we have not seen each other in weeks. This simple discipline reminds us to not take each other for granted. Due to the complexity of life, it is easy to put my wife on the back burner and forget about her. However, sooner or later, if I have left her on the back burner too long, the smoke rises, and something begins to burn and stink.

Just like all relationships, it's easy to put Jesus on the back burner and forget about him too. This is precisely why Jesus was writing the church in Ephesus. The smoke was rising, and something was beginning to burn and stink. It didn't take long for Jesus to smell the stench, so he called his disciples to revive and return with a deeper kind of love.

Effortless Love

"I love you," is easy to say, but not necessarily easy to do. When we slow down and think about whether or not our love for Jesus is verbalized, we might discover many things, including good things, are competing for our affections. Our friends, hobbies, sporting events, work, ministry, and even our loved ones can compete with Jesus and a kingdom-oriented lifestyle.

Allowing Jesus to be first and foremost in our life can be quite challenging. In fact, this reality is typically the reason people slowly separate from God's way of life. However, the beautiful thing is, once we begin placing Jesus first and foremost, we can truly love everything else around us. We cannot completely understand and express love until we first experience God's unending love for us. In a unique way, God's unconditional love produces the ability to love ourselves and those around us with a pure and selfless kind of love.

If we are not careful, or if we are like the church in Ephesus, we can quickly fall into the trap of trying to love God and love others out of our own ability. Eventually, these attempts at love will become a form of performing love, and this type of love is difficult, if not impossible, to sustain over the long haul.

The Ephesian church was doing a lot of good things, but they were on the verge of burnout. They were trying to love out of their own willpower, instead of experiencing an empowering and effortless love from the one who shows us how to love well.

In order to help the church in Ephesus see this distinction, Jesus used the image of a "lampstand" to communicate the church's proper posture (Rev. 2:5). The Jewish lampstand is a central image within the book of Revelation. Jesus is "the light of the world" (John 8:12; 9:5), and the church is to be the stand which holds up and supports the Light.[8]

When Jesus declared he would remove the Ephesian church's lampstand, he was also stating he would remove himself, his presence, from their community. Some theologians have understood the removal of the Ephesian church from its place (Rev. 2:5) as an allusion to the silt deposits of the Cayster River which eventually forced the literal relocation of the city.[9] No longer would the church in Ephesus be influential in the culture at large and within their network of churches. The light would fade out if they chose to not remain disciplined and intentional in their love.

Discipline

We may not like the sound of the word *discipline* very much—it tends to stir up images of schoolwork, diets, or workout routines. However, it is important to know the word *disciple* is the root word for discipline.

Disciples who choose to remain fully devoted to Jesus understand discipline as a good thing—a very good thing. They are willing to put into practice certain life patterns and habits which continually realign their lives to the essence of Jesus.

In order to excel in anything, discipline is required. This is true for athletes, musicians, electricians, accountants, and disciples of Jesus. Effective discipline is not drudgery—it is delightful. Of course, training has difficult aspects, but the hard work pays off when we bask in the enjoyment of the results. Just watch a master violinist and notice how he or she is not straining to perform, but simply moving to the music.

Discipline comes in the form of training. Training for something is enabling us to do what we haven't yet been able to do by our own direct effort. Trying is not enough. First Timothy 4:7 could be paraphrased this way: "Don't try. Train!" When it comes to our spiritual training, it is important to know our regimen is connecting us with a power, the Holy Spirit, which is much greater than our own willpower.

Discipline also works by helping us develop new habits. We can't be good at any sport or musical expression without developing a number of technical habits with our body.

The spiritual life works the same way. If we want to grow in our relationship with God, we need new habits and practices, engaging our mind and heart with God. This is why it is important to train by meditating on Scripture, praying for our enemies, or reaching out to the poor and oppressed. Engaging in strategic spiritual disciplines will keep us on the right path, moving us in the right direction.

In his book *The Spirit of the Disciplines*, Dallas Willard described several disciplines which can help us remain committed to Jesus and his loving presence. Willard packages these disciplines in two categories: (1) the disciplines of abstinence—ways of denying ourselves something we want or need in order to make space to focus on and connect with God—and (2) the disciplines of engagement—ways of connecting with God and other people, communicating honestly with them in order to love and be loved.

Take a moment and reflect on Willard's list and consider implementing some new revival habits in your life:

The Disciplines of Abstinence

Solitude: Refraining from interacting with other people in order to be alone with God and be found by him.

Silence: Not speaking in order to quiet our whole self and lean into God's presence.

Fasting: Going without food (or something we consistently turn to) for a period of intense prayer.

Sabbath: Doing no work for pay in order to rest in God's person and provision; praying and playing with God and others.

Secrecy: Not making our good deeds or qualities known, letting God or others receive attention and to find our completeness in God alone.

Submission: Humbling ourselves in order to come under the authority, wisdom, and power of Jesus Christ as our Lord and Master.[10]

The Disciplines of Engagement

Bible Reading: Trusting the Spirit-inspired words of Scripture as our guide, wisdom, and strength for life.

Worship: Praising God for his greatness, goodness, and beauty in words, music, ritual, or silence.

Prayer: Conversing with God about what we're experiencing and doing together.

Soul Friendship: Engaging other disciples of Jesus in uplifting conversations or other spiritual practices.

Personal Reflection: Paying attention to our inner self in order to grow in love for God, others, and self.

Service: Humbly serving God by overflowing with his love and compassion to others, especially those in need.[11]

To be sure, there is no complete list of spiritual disciplines. Any activity helping a person follow Jesus better might be acceptable. I like to consider fishing with my boys a spiritual discipline.

Jesus himself practiced all of these spiritual disciplines, including fishing with his boys, and he challenged his followers to do what he did. Like Jesus modeled, as we engage in these spiritual disciplines, we must keep in mind they are simply a means to help us be with Jesus and to become more like him. They do not earn us anything. We do the disciplines because we long to be closer to Jesus.

A Natural

In the eighteenth century, a young Russian man wanted to know if it was possible to pray without ceasing, as the Bible commanded. He asked an old monk, who told him truly ceaseless prayer comes in quieting the mind and making the mind one with the heart. He gave the young man these words: "Lord Jesus Christ, have mercy on me," and told him to pray them three thousand times a day. When the man completed the task, the monk advised him to pray the same prayer six thousand times, and then later, twelve thousand times a day, until it became almost like breathing.[12]

Now, this spiritual discipline may not sound very realistic to do, but the point of all the disciplines is to do it so much that it flows naturally from our lives and we don't even have to think about it.

Imagine being Johann Sebastian Bach for a moment. Think about all of those countless hours he spent banging on the keys of his piano and scribbling with his quill, as he composed some of the world's greatest musical textures and cantatas. Bach wasn't born a natural musician—he was simply willing to train himself to the point where everything he did felt natural.

The same should be true about disciples of Jesus. We should be able to train ourselves in the way of Jesus, so everything we do feels natural and people might just say, "That person loves God and loves others so well they kind of remind me of Jesus."

For the church in Ephesus, victory or conquering (Rev. 2:7) required more than hard work and theological soundness—it required unifying love.[13] A church where love ceases can no longer function properly as a local expression of Christ's body. Some churches may die from lack of outreach, lack of planning for the emerging generations, or lack of hospitality to visitors, but Jesus wanted the church in Ephesus to know they are on the verge of dying because of their lack of love for God and how they were treating people.

Interestingly, at the end of the letter, Jesus reflected back on the original "tree of life" metaphor (Gen. 3:22) and reminded the church of their source of eternal life. The reward for overcoming and remaining disciplined in unifying love is the privilege of eating from the tree of life in God's garden or paradise (Rev. 2:7), a familiar image in ancient Judaism.

Jesus seemed to be alluding to the fact that the Ephesian church was on the verge of being removed from the garden of Eden, similar to how Adam and Eve were removed from the garden because of their disobedience. However, if the church in Ephesus returned to loving God and others, they could rest in the promise of enjoying the fruit of God's garden forever.

If we want to experience personal revival and remain in God's garden, let's begin by reaffirming Jesus' words in Matthew 22:37–39: "'*Love* the Lord your God with all your heart and with all your soul and with all your mind.' This is the first and greatest commandment. And the second is like it: '*Love* your neighbor as yourself'" (emphasis added).

Discussion Questions

- Make a list of your actions last week. What took priority? What consumed your mind when you first woke up and went to sleep? What might you need to reprioritize in order to keep Christ first and foremost?

- Over time, the church in Ephesus moved from an offensive posture of proactive love to a defensive posture of merely protecting the mission of God. Is your life properly balanced between an offensive posture of love and a defensive posture of protecting the mission of God? Which side do you need to rebalance?

- In your daily life, do you find the essence of Christ intertwined and interlaced within your conversations and daily routines? What spiritual disciplines might you be able to implement in order to develop a consistent devotion for God?

2 | Smyrna
Faithful and Fearless

*My desire is to live more to God today than yesterday
and to be more holy this hour than the last.*
—Francis Asbury

I have always enjoyed the game of basketball. I may not have the pep in my step like I once did, but I still try to play as much as I can. Recently, I was in the middle of a competitive game and I crashed the boards to gather a rebound. As I was mid-air, simultaneously my teammate was attempting to swat the ball out to the top of the key. Instead of swatting the ball, he missed and smacked me square in my eye. I quickly collapsed to the floor in agonizing pain. I had never been hit that hard before in my life. I laid helplessly on the floor for a couple of minutes, trying to regain my composure. After a few minutes, I was finally able to roll off of the court, still wallowing in my pain.

The blow to my eye socket left me uncomfortable for days. I had what seemed to be a never-ending headache, my vision was blurry, and I was left with an embarrassing bloodshot eye for more than a month. It was a dreadful experience and I hope it never happens again.

As humans, we dislike suffering and we try to do everything possible to avoid pain. Yet, sometimes accidents happen, and we are forced to endure the pain.

I have experienced plenty of pain from playing basketball, especially after I entered my forties. Sometimes I wonder about giving up the sport, but it's the only sport I truly love. I have discovered it's easier to endure pain when it's connected to something I love.

Most of us haven't had to experience physical pain because of our faith in Jesus. We can't fathom someone smacking us in the eye simply because we believe in Jesus.

Modern-day Americans are free to worship wherever, whenever, and whomever. To think about a world where an individual is required to suffer for his or her faith is almost incomprehensible. Even today, it is estimated nearly 159,000 people die each year across the globe because they will not renounce their faith in Christ.[1]

Take a moment and ponder this question: *If I were being persecuted and tortured for my faith, would I remain faithful to Christ, or would I buckle under the pressure and deny Christ?*

In the first century, being a part of a church community was not about liking the particular personality of a pastor, enjoying the sermon, or taking pleasure in the worship music. It was about staying alive and encouraging your friends to continue living in the kingdom of God on earth.

Being a part of a church in the first century took on a whole new meaning and purpose. The broader church network was a must-have ingredient in a person's life if he or she wanted to remain a faithful follower of Christ.

Let's turn to the second letter of Revelation, which was written to the church in Smyrna, who knew all too well about the cost of being a disciple of Jesus:

"Write this letter to the angel of the church in Smyrna. This is the message from the one who is the First and the Last, who was dead but is now alive:

"I know about your suffering and your poverty—but you are rich! I know the blasphemy of those opposing you. They say they are Jews, but they are not, because their synagogue belongs to Satan. Don't be afraid of what you are about to suffer. The devil will throw some of you into prison to test you. You will suffer for ten days. But if you remain faithful even when facing death, I will give you the crown of life.

"Anyone with ears to hear must listen to the Spirit and understand what he is saying to the churches. Whoever is victorious will not be harmed by the second death." (Rev. 2:8–11 NLT)

Smyrna 101

If it was inevitable for Ephesus to come first in the list of the seven churches, then it was only natural for Smyrna to come in second. For three centuries, Smyrna had been one of the most important cities in Asia Minor. Like Ephesus, Smyrna was an important center of the imperial cult, and was the second city to receive this privilege from the Roman emperor.[2]

Even more, of all the ancient cities, Smyrna was known as the loveliest. Roman historians often described Smyrna as a flower, a rainbow, and a city reaching up to the heavens.[3]

There was one period, however, when Smyrna was considered dead. Around 600 BC, Smyrna was destroyed by the king of Lydia and remained desolate for about three hundred years. Smyrna rose from the dead when a ruler refounded it in 290 BC. By the time the first century rolled around, Smyrna was fully revived and had become one of the busiest commercial centers and economic hubs within the Roman province of Asia.[4]

Smyrna had maintained loyalties to Rome from a very early date. In 195 BC, a cultic temple was built to honor the goddess Roma. In addition, Smyrna was given the privilege of erecting a temple to the Roman emperor Tiberius, beckoning people to come from all over the region to worship his image.

Smyrna was also a center for the worship of Cybele, another one of the Greek gods peppering the Roman world. The Temple of Cybele was at the shore of the Aegean Sea, where Smyrna's Golden Street began.[5] Along the street there were magnificent temples dedicated to Apollo, Asclepius, Aphrodite, and Zeus. As you can imagine, this street was quite awe-inspiring, kind of like Times Square in New York.

In the letter, Jesus mentioned how he was very aware of those who were opposed to the Christ-followers in Smyrna (Rev. 2:9). Smyrna had a large Jewish population which appeared to maintain intense hostility toward Christians. Rome knew Jews were monotheistic and were an ancient, ethnic religion that merited tolerance. The recognition that Christians were a part of Judaism thus protected Christians (at least initially) from unnecessary persecution. Unfortunately, many Jewish synagogue leaders seemed to have felt it necessary to distinguish themselves sharply from Christians or even to make the Jewish Christians unwelcome in the synagogues.[6]

Since the Jewish community in Smyrna was substantial, they seemed to have been on more positive terms with the Roman government, which may explain why these Jewish leaders didn't want to associate with the Jewish Christians. The Jewish leaders needed to continue receiving favorable positioning from Rome and were probably nervous about being associated with messianic movements like Christianity.[7]

Because of Smyrna's strong historic ties to Rome; its worship of many gods, goddesses, and Roman emperors; and the hostility of the Jewish community, it was not easy for disciples of Jesus to remain faithful to the mission of God. For example, in AD 156, when Polycarp, the bishop of Smyrna, was martyred, it was the Jewish leaders who were instrumental in his arrest and execution.[8]

In Revelation 2:10, Jesus counseled the church in Smyrna to not be afraid and he let them know suffering for their faith would be inevitable. It is interesting to note a distinction between being faithful and being successful. Observant Christ-followers would be wise to examine the dynamics of what success looked like for the church in Smyrna. Being faithful in the midst of opposition is success in Jesus' mind; however, all too often, a church nowadays is labeled successful if it feels like it has material plenty, power in numbers, and prosperity to boot.

Jesus also mentioned how the synagogue, the Jewish place of worship and education, was associated with Satan, and the Devil would be involved in throwing Christians into prison to test them (vv. 9–10).

As far as the first-century Jews were concerned, the early Christians were a heretical sect. To them, the Christians were misguided and believed in the wrong Messiah. Therefore, they were strongly contested, and in the Jewish mind, life would have been better if Christians were nonexistent. As far as the Romans were concerned, the Christians were just another Jewish sect, and as long as the Christians did not stir up any trouble, they were more than happy to include their spirituality in the Roman pluralistic way of life.[9]

Since the Jews had developed animosity toward Christians and had disassociated themselves with the Christian movement, they had become anti-Christ and would have been considered the present-day personification of Satan, an adversary of God. In other words, because the Jews were persecuting God's new work on earth, the Jews had unknowingly become an instrument of Satan. Many commentators thus recognize the likelihood that at least some of the members of the local Jewish community were collaborating with local Roman officials to oppress the Christian minority.[10]

The Romans tolerated all religions and cults; however, if a particular sect became disruptive, swift action was taken. If the Jews brought about disruptive charges against the early Christians, which they did, then the Roman officials would have been considered anti-Christ. It was typical in the first century for the Roman officials, a tool of the Devil, to hold people in prison for a short period of time in order to investigate the situation and discern what kind of action needed to be taken. Those who were in prison would be tested and usually tortured in the process in an attempt to secure information against others.[11] The very knowledge that imprisonment could include such torture demanded faithfulness from the Christians in Smyrna.

A New Kind of Prosperity

As you can imagine, the early Christ-followers in any Roman city lived in a constant state of struggle, both socially and economically. They were living in cities where one's wealth determined one's worth. Yet life on earth was not prosperous for Jesus' first and second generations of disciples. Life was extremely difficult and there were no guarantees from one day to the next.

Nevertheless, Jesus noted how the faithful and fearless in Smyrna would receive the "crown of life" (Rev. 2:10 NLT). As with all of the images and metaphors within the seven letters, these images connect to the essence of the particular city being addressed.

Behind the city of Smyrna, there rose the Pagos, a hill covered with temples and noble buildings, which were spoken of as the Crown of Smyrna. One historian described the glorious hill as "a queenly city crowned with towers." It was also said that the Smyrnaean "Street of Gold" was the necklace around the hill.[12]

Even more, crowns (wreaths of olive, laurel, pine, or celery) were commonly distributed to victors in battle and more often given to champions in athletic competitions; hence, the reason a crown would have been a familiar symbolic image of victory to everyone in Smyrna. Jesus wanted his faithful disciples to know his alternative "crown of life" would be far more glorious than anything a worldly, God-less city could offer.

Many people have been killed for their faith throughout the ages. These people are referred to as martyrs. It's interesting to note, the Greek word for *martyr* is translated in the New Testament as *witness*.

In Acts 1:8, when Jesus said, "You will be my *witnesses* [*martyres*] in Jerusalem, and in all Judea and Samaria, and to the ends of the earth," there is a much deeper meaning behind this mandate. This does not mean every follower of Christ should try to be killed for their faith, but it does suggest being a witness for Jesus may require some level of suffering and, potentially, death.

In fact, if we have not prepared ourselves and our twenty-first-century churches to die for Christ's name if necessary, we have not completed our responsibility of preparing disciples. One time, Jesus told a crowd of potential disciples:

"If any of you wants to be my follower, you must give up your own way, take up your cross, and follow me. If you try to hang on to your life, you will lose it. But if you *give up your life* for my sake and for the sake of the Good News, you will save it. And what do you benefit if you gain the whole world but lose your own soul? Is anything worth more than your soul? If anyone is ashamed of me and my message in these adulterous and sinful days, the Son of Man will be ashamed of that person when he returns in the glory of his Father with the holy angels." (Mark 8:34–38 NLT, emphasis added)

Without knowing some of the martyrdom stories of the past, we may fall prey to the comfortable-Christian syndrome, or worse yet, assume Jesus primarily sacrificed his life in order to make us happy and trouble-free in this life. Let's take a moment and journey into the stories of a few inspiring souls who went down in history as faithful and fearless.

Examples of Christian Martyrs

Stephen

Chapters 6 and 7 in the book of Acts provide us with the detailed account of Stephen's martyrdom. Stephen is considered the first Christian martyr after Christ himself.

Stephen was speaking the truth of Jesus Christ; however, his words offended his listeners. Stephen's opposition put together a council which brought false witness to the things Stephen was saying (Acts 6:11–13). Stephen proclaimed God's own people, the Jewish people, were at fault for not listening to Jesus' call to righteousness. The Jewish leaders' reaction was to lash out, and they ran Stephen out of the city and stoned him to death.

Stephen patiently accepted the persecution that was given to him. Before Stephen's final death blow, he asked the Lord not to hold those who stoned him guilty and essentially repeated Christ's words on the cross: "'Lord Jesus, receive my spirit.' Then he fell on his knees and cried out, 'Lord, do not hold this sin against them'" (Acts 7:59–60).[13]

Andrew

Andrew was one of the first disciples of Jesus. He was previously a disciple of John the Baptist (John 1:40), but began following Jesus when Jesus called him to be one of his twelve disciples (Matt. 4:18–20). Andrew was also the brother of the animated Peter. Post-biblical records inform us Andrew went on to preach around the Black Sea and was influential in starting several churches. He was also the founder of the church in Byzantium (or Constantinople).

Tradition asserts Andrew was crucified on an X-shaped cross on the northern coast of Peloponnese. As the story goes, Andrew refused to be crucified in the same manner as Christ because he did not feel worthy of dying in the same way of his Lord and Master.[14]

Peter

Peter is known as the disciple who spoke before he thought. After Jesus' death, Peter was the fiery preacher prominently seen in the first half of the book of Acts. Peter founded the church in Antioch and traveled around the countryside preaching mainly to Jews about Jesus.

Peter was martyred under Caesar Nero's reign. He was killed in Rome between the years AD 64 and 67. Tradition holds Peter was crucified upside down. Like Andrew, his brother, Peter is said to have refused to be crucified in the same manner as Christ because he was unworthy to be executed in the same way as his Lord and Master.[15]

Polycarp

As with many people in the early centuries, Polycarp's exact birth and death dates are not known. Even his date of martyrdom is disputed. Presumably, Polycarp died somewhere between AD 155 and 167. He was most likely a disciple of the apostle John who wrote several books of the Bible. Polycarp may have been one of the chief people responsible for compiling the New Testament.

Because of Polycarp's refusal to burn incense to the Roman emperor, he was sentenced to burn at the stake. Polycarp stood for the Lord Jesus Christ all the way to the end, despite the efforts to persuade him to renounce Christ. One of the judges tried to get him to deny his faith by saying, "Reverence thy old age . . . Swear by Caesar's Fortune. Repent, and renounce Christ."

It is at this point, Polycarp gave his famous response: "Eighty and six years have I now served Christ, and he has never done me the least wrong. How, then, can I blaspheme my King and my Savior?"

The judge then angrily urged him to swear by the genius of Caesar. Yet Polycarp refused, and offered to share his faith in Christ.

After several attempts to coerce him to renounce Christ, the Roman officials finally took Polycarp to the stake with plans to nail him to the beam. Polycarp spoke up and said, "Let me alone as I am: For he who has given me strength to endure the fire, will also enable me, without your securing me by nails, to stand without moving in the pile." The officials proceeded to tie him to the stake to face his death.[16]

John Wycliffe

Known as the "Morning Star of the Reformation," John Wycliffe was a fourteenth-century theologian. Wycliffe is probably best remembered as a translator of the Holy Scriptures, believing the Bible should be available to people in their common language. Wycliffe translated the Latin Vulgate into common English, which was considered an inconceivable action by the papal authority.

While Wycliffe was not burned at the stake as a martyr, his persecution extended beyond his death. Wycliffe's body was exhumed and burned along with many of his writings. The Anti-Wycliffe Statute of AD 1401 brought persecution to his followers and specifically addressed the fact that there should not be any translation of Scripture into common languages.[17]

Jim Elliot

Jim Elliot and four of his missionary friends were killed on January 8, 1956, while trying to establish contact with the Auca Indians in Ecuador (now known as the Waodani people). Jim Elliot, Nate Saint, Ed McCully, Pete Fleming, and Roger Youderian had been working to make friendly contact with the Auca tribe, which they had seen from an airplane window. Though they had only met one tribesman face-to-face, they had participated in trades with the Auca from a plane to ground system. When Elliot and his friends landed on a river beach on that fateful January day, they were slaughtered by the waiting men.

Their deaths were not in vain, though. Their widows continued to make peaceful contact with the Auca people and, eventually, won the hearts of the tribe.[18]

Nag Hammadi Massacre

On the night of January 7, 2010, a group of eight Egyptian Christians were killed as they left their church after celebrating a Christmas mass in Nag Hammadi, Egypt. The motive behind the massacre is disputed, but it was carried out by a militant Islamic tribe. It may have been done in retaliation for an alleged crime against a Muslim girl by a Christian man. Even if that was the reason, the retaliation was not targeted at the man who committed the crime, but at Christians because of their association through their religious affiliation.[19]

Crowns of Glory

In this life, a disciple's loyalty may bring a crown of thorns, but in the life to come, it will surely bring a crown of glory.

The first-century story of Smyrna is the story of so many who have attempted to participate in the mandate of Jesus to be his witnesses throughout the world (Acts 1:8).

Jesus' message to the church in Smyrna reminds us how suffering and hardship should be expected within the Christian life. Christians in the twenty-first century may be less likely to experience physical torture because of their faith, but the history of Christian persecution provides us with a deeper understanding of what it means to remain faithful to Christ. The persecuted believers of the past prompt us to consider the way of Christ as something more than merely another pathway to personal happiness—it truly is a pathway to eternal life.

Discussion Questions

- What are your greatest fears in life?

- What is the Holy Spirit saying to you about your fears?

- What is your action plan to overcome those fears?

- How do the stories of persecuted Christians throughout history affect your faith-perspective today?

3 | **Pergamum**

Loyal and Listening

> *The best measure of a spiritual life is not its*
> *ecstasies, but its obedience.*
> —Oswald Chambers

On one peaceful Saturday night a few of my high school buddies thought it would be fun to camp out at a public campground near a river bend. We were sitting around, minding our own business, when a group of rowdies suddenly came blasting into the campground. They pulled up next to our cars, set up camp, and popped open their beers. After a while, the group started to mill over toward my friends and me.

We were gracious and entertained them with some small talk. During the course of the conversation, one of my friends mentioned what high school we were from and the fact that we all played on the football team.

Little did we know, we were talking with the football players of our rival school. Apparently, the top jock's car had recently been keyed by some people from our school. As you can imagine, the conversation started to escalate.

Soon, voices were being raised and fingers were being pointed. I was standing there, kind of shocked, wondering why these fellows were so worked up. All of the sudden, one of the linemen stepped in front of me and threw a round-house punch to my face.

I went down hard. As I struggled to regain my composure, I noticed all the rivals were closing in on me and all my buddies were running away.

Fearing a severe beating, I jumped up and ran out into the river. They stopped chasing me at the shoreline, so I was safe for the moment. I proceeded to float downstream and hung out by myself on the shoreline for a while. Once it got dark, I started walking through the campsite, searching for my friends. However, they were nowhere to be found and their cars were gone.

I sneakily crept up to my car undetected and headed home. When I saw my friends at school the next day, I let them have it! "Why didn't you stick up for me? Why didn't you have my back? I can't believe you guys!" I yelled. They mumbled some sort of an apology, but they had already proven themselves to be disloyal.

Loyalty is a quality all of us desire in a friendship and it is, without a doubt, the foundation for any life-giving relationship—including our relationship with God.

At the core, believing in God is not merely about agreeing to a certain set of principles and doctrines (although those things are very important); it is about agreeing to enter into a relationship with God, through Jesus Christ. It is not about knowing *of* God; it is about *knowing* God and God *knowing* us. This distinction is central to our faith, especially if we want to avoid the branding of legalistic religion.

The challenging question for disciples of Jesus is: Do we have what it takes to remain loyal to King Jesus, even when life gets difficult?

This is the underlying question within the third letter of the book of Revelation. Let's take a moment and peer into the church of Pergamum and discover what their relationship with Jesus looked like:

> "Write this letter to the angel of the church in Pergamum. This is the message from the one with the sharp two-edged sword:
>
> "I know that you live in the city where Satan has his throne, yet you have remained loyal to me. You

refused to deny me even when Antipas, my faithful witness, was martyred among you there in Satan's city.

"But I have a few complaints against you. You tolerate some among you whose teaching is like that of Balaam, who showed Balak how to trip up the people of Israel. He taught them to sin by eating food offered to idols and by committing sexual sin. In a similar way, you have some Nicolaitans among you who follow the same teaching. Repent of your sin, or I will come to you suddenly and fight against them with the sword of my mouth.

"Anyone with ears to hear must listen to the Spirit and understand what he is saying to the churches. To everyone who is victorious I will give some of the manna that has been hidden away in heaven. And I will give to each one a white stone, and on the stone will be engraved a new name that no one understands except the one who receives it." (Rev. 2:12–17 NLT)

Pergamum 101

In the first century, the city of Pergamum had a prominent place within the Roman Empire. For a long period of time, Pergamum was the capital city of the province of Asia and was considered one of the most famous cities in the region, boasting 120,000–200,000 inhabitants.[1] There were many reasons for Pergamum's fame.

First, Pergamum was one of the great religious centers within the Roman Empire. In particular, it had two famous shrines. In the letter, Pergamum was said to be home of Satan's "throne" (Rev. 2:13). Obviously, this is a reference to something the early Christ-followers thought was evil and in direct opposition to the purposes of God in the world.

Since Pergamum was the capital city, it collected many Greek altars and temples. In memory of the great victory of 240 BC, the city erected a great altar to the Greek god Zeus in front of the Temple of Athena, which stood eight hundred feet up on Pergamum's grand hill. At forty feet high, the altar stood on a projecting ledge of rock and appeared like a great throne overlooking the city. All day the shrine smoked from the burnt sacrifices offered to "Zeus the Savior," whose sculptures included serpents.[2] Many scholars have suggested this great throne was Jesus' reference point to Satan's "throne."[3]

Second, Pergamum was intricately connected to the worship of another god named Asclepius. The Temple of Asclepius also doubled as a Roman hospital, and the sick would flock to the priests of Asclepius for healing remedies and various forms of ancient psychotherapy. The most famous title for Asclepius was "The Savior," and the symbol for Asclepius was also a serpent.[4]

Third, and possibly most important, the city of Pergamum was one of the major centers for Caesar worship. In 29 BC, Caesar Augustus permitted the building of a temple to himself and the goddess of Roma in Pergamum. This was one of the first locations where the Roman emperor (Caesar) demanded worship of himself.[5] The Temple of Augustus stood on the lofty rock citadel, clearly visible to anyone who approached the city.[6]

There are likely multiple reasons why Jesus referred to Pergamum as the place where "Satan has his throne" (v. 13). Because of the centrality of Zeus, Asclepius, and the worship of the supposedly divine Caesars of the day, Pergamum Christians found it extremely difficult to remain loyal to Christ.

Even more, Jesus' disciples in Pergamum were also witnesses of the forceful power of Rome. Christians in Pergamum had been witnesses of the death of faithful Antipas, who had died by the swipe of a Roman sword (v. 13). In the Roman world, the sword was a symbol of power and authority. Interestingly, Jesus referred to himself as the one holding the "double-edged sword" (v. 12), which could be interpreted as Jesus embodying double the power and authority of Rome.

The image of the sword may also allude to the Roman government's right to execute capital punishment; in which case, Jesus was reminding Christians that he, not the Roman governor, ultimately holds the power of life and death (Rev. 1:18).[7]

Tension

Christians of Pergamum faced adversity each time they walked through their city. They lived with constant pressure to bend to the alternative religious forces.

Jesus referred to Antipas as his faithful martyr (Rev. 2:13). In life and death, Antipas was a loyal witness for Jesus. To be sure, the faith of Antipas was rooted in something much deeper than superficial forms of Christianity. Antipas was an incredible testimony of someone who was willing to remain committed to Christ even in the face of death.

The church in Pergamum found itself in a culture where many external pressures abounded. In such a situation, the people of the church had a choice: they could either give up their allegiance to Christ or they could remain loyal.

Bear in mind, Jesus does not like people straddling the fence of commitment. Jesus' followers are either with him or not.

Commitment and Couches

If there is one thing our culture needs these days, it would be an injection of loyalty. Loyalty to others is a dying attribute in our world. Businesses let go of employees after years of loyal service. Divorce is at an all-time high. Cheating on a spouse has become somewhat trendy. Even our celebrities and politicians we hold in high esteem have proven to be disloyal to their lovers.

Remember the dramatic breakup of Tom Cruise and Katie Holmes? It was not that long ago we witnessed Tom Cruise jumping up and down on Oprah's couch proclaiming his unending love for Katie. I guess she didn't "complete" him.[8]

Many twenty-somethings are scared to commit to any long-term relationship. Nowadays, according to Brides.com, the average age of marriage for men is 29.8.[9] There seems to be an underlying skepticism of anyone who claims to want loyalty in a relationship.

Do you see the problem?

People are trying to build relationships without loyalty.

Jesus knew that any relationship, including ours with him, would only last if it was built on the foundation of loyalty. This is why Jesus was constantly testing and celebrating the allegiance of his disciples.

Without a doubt, loyalty is one of the central virtues within the Christian life. Followers of Christ must never enter into a relationship with God with an escape route or prenuptial agreement in mind; it will simply not work.

Fine Lines

For the most part, the church in Pergamum was a community of loyal followers; however, Jesus had a few complaints against them. The main complaint dealt with how they tolerated the teachings of some of the misguided leaders within their mix. The problem with their false teachings was not that they denied the role of Jesus in their spirituality, but they taught a message of permissible grace.

Permissible grace is really no grace at all. Permissible grace claims a person is free to indulge in the sinful nature and blend their spirituality with the culture around them. This idea is clearly opposed to Jesus' teachings of dying to one's self, taking up their cross (an execution beam) and following Christ daily (Luke 9:23).

Specifically, Jesus referenced the fact that the church in Pergamum allowed the teachings of Balaam and the Nicolaitans to circulate in their gatherings (Rev. 2:14–15). "Balaam" is likely not the explicit name of a teacher, but a code name signifying that this teacher is a false one, leading astray the people of God. In the Bible and Jewish tradition, Balaam acted out of greed for money (Deut. 23:4–5). He led Israel into sin in order to take them out of God's favor, recognizing this was the only way to destroy them (Num. 31:16). The particular sins of

Israel in connection with Balaam were sexual immorality and food offered to idols.[10]

When Jesus highlighted the teaching of Balaam, he was clearly referencing the church's tendency to promote syncretism, which is a form of compromised theology. Christians in Pergamum would have been tempted to engage in pagan festivals and eat free food that had been sacrificed to idols and Caesar. This type of cultural involvement around pagan festivals presented Christians with difficult choices. Interestingly, by the early second century, Roman officials recognized Christian influence in refusal to eat sacrificial meat and responded harshly.[11]

Throughout the gospel narratives, Jesus adamantly proclaimed following him came with a cost (Luke 10:3). To think we can do whatever we please and still be in a right relationship with God misses the entire point of his transformational grace.

Jesus' transformational grace causes us to think hard about our actions at home, at work, or when we are hanging out with friends. The author of James takes God's transforming grace to another level when he reminds us: "If anyone, then, knows the good they ought to do and doesn't do it, it is sin for them" (4:17). Simply put, God's grace should always stir us into action.

Following Through

One of the things that has helped me overcome my disloyal impulses is to focus on my follow-through. In basketball, one's follow-through, the flick of the wrist after a shot, is the most important part of the shot. If the follow-through is cut short, the shot has little chance of making it into the bucket. Follow-through may be the last 10 percent of the shot, but it determines everything.

In my relationship with God, I've come to realize the importance of following through. Making sure I give God my last 10 percent should be my focus. I'm certainly guilty of being proud of the fact that I gave God an initial 90 percent. I mean, 90-percent loyalty is good, right? Well, if we're being honest, even with 90-percent loyalty, we probably missed the shot.

One thing is for sure, I have missed a lot of shots in the game of life. When I do miss, I'm grateful I have a great coach that doesn't grind me down and make me feel like a loser. My coach, Jesus, simply whispers: "I love you. You got this. Get back out there, but this time I want you to follow through."

I've come to learn, when I feel like my follow-through and loyalty is weak, I don't need to do more. What I need to do is pause and listen.

It's interesting to note, all of John's seven letters end with this phrase: "Anyone with ears to hear must *listen* to the Spirit and understand what he is saying to the churches" (Rev. 2:11 NLT, emphasis added).

Listening to God's voice has everything to do with remaining loyal.

Manna and White Stones

For Christians in Pergamum, Jesus' encouragement to overcome meant that they would continue being loyal, even while they faced opposition and stood against false teachers (Rev. 2:13–16). To those who would overcome, Jesus promised the "hidden manna" and a "white stone with a new name written on it" (v. 17).

The hidden manna likely alludes to the manna distributed to God's faithful people during the first exodus under Moses' leadership (Ex. 16:4). For Christians in the first century, this reminder of God's provision of promised manna also contrasts starkly with the idolatrous pagan food for which Balaam's followers seemed prepared to compromise.[12]

The image of the white stone could have a few origins. One option could be the sharp contrast with the black stone distributed as a token for those who worshiped Cybele, the prominent Phrygian Mother Goddess. Another option could be how people used small stones as admission tokens for public assemblies or festivities, which may symbolize the celebration of the new heavenly reign, fully expressed later in John's revelation of Jesus Christ (Rev. 21). Or, perhaps, the white stone is a reference to some ancient courtrooms, where jurors voted for acquittal with a white stone and for conviction with a black stone.[13]

Even more, the color white contains an important dynamic to consider. Although most building materials in Pergamum were of dark brown granite, this particular city used white marble for its inscriptions. Jesus wanted his overcomers to know their inscription was engraved in white, which is also a symbol of eternal life and purity from sin used throughout Revelation.

The inscription of an overcomer's "new name" is also an important detail (Rev. 2:17). It was common for other pagan deities to give worshipers new names to signify a new identity, just as parents named children shortly after birth.[14] In Israel's own history, a change of name was often associated with a promise (see Gen. 17:5). Jesus' new name is likely alluding to Isaiah 62:2, when the prophet Isaiah said, "The nations will see your righteousness. World leaders will be blinded by your glory. And you will be given a *new name* by the LORD's own mouth" (NLT, emphasis added). Jesus' new name, "known only to the [person] who receives it," (Rev. 2:17) is representative of a new description of a person's new identity in the kingdom of God.

To be sure, a lot of modern Christianity has become indistinguishable from our culture. In our attempt to persuade the world that we are relevant, we can be tempted to morph into the values of the world rather than the values of the kingdom of God. However, even with all the tensions, God's loyal overcomers can still rise up with an uncompromising witness for Christ. It is easier for Christians to avoid compromising God's values when we keep in mind the much better world God has in store for us right now and for all eternity.

Whatever we must overcome, in order to stay alive in Christ, we must remember our new name engraved on the white stone!

Discussion Questions

- In what settings do you have the most difficulty remaining loyal to Jesus?

- If you are unable to remove yourself from difficult settings, how can you remain loyal within those surroundings?

- Busyness is one of the greatest enemies of listening to Jesus. What are some ways you can become less busy and create more space for listening to God's voice?

- What elements do you need in order to assist your listening capacity? Do you need music? Do you need time in the great outdoors? Do you need something visual? Do you need people around you? Do you need solitude?

4 | Thyatira

Improving and Intentional

> *Have you noticed how much praying for revival has been going on of late—and how little revival has resulted? I believe the problem is that we have been trying to substitute praying for obeying, and it simply will not work. To pray for revival while ignoring the plain precept laid down in Scripture is to waste a lot of words and get nothing for our trouble. Prayer will become effective when we stop using it as a substitute for obedience.*
>
> —A. W. Tozer

If I had a dollar for every time I had to discipline my kids, I'd be a wealthy man. My wife and I are constantly teaching, correcting, and persuading our kids to get along, forgive, and speak kindly to each other. Is that too much to ask? We love our children dearly, and because of our love, we will not settle for mediocrity or complacency within our household.

As parents, we not only see our children—we see the potential in them. We long for them to be the best they can possibly be. This means when we see attitudes or behaviors from our children which are less than what we expect from them, we must sit them down and have a talk. In our talks, we mention lessons from the Bible, ask them emotional awareness questions, and then encourage them in a new God-honoring perspective. We hope our talks (and re-talks) lead to inner transformation. While external changes are appreciated, what we really long to see is internal improvement.

Improvement is something we all desire in every facet of life. In our homes, workplaces, governmental agencies, churches, and relationships, we innately long for things to progressively become better.

Jesus held this type of improvement-oriented perspective too. Throughout life, Jesus always wants us to grow and improve. In the process of growing in our relationship with God, there should always be an underlying sense of progress.

Remember, like parenting, discipleship is not only about behavior modification (the external change); it is also about behavior "moldification" (the internal change). When we sign up to be a disciple of Jesus, we are willing to submit to Jesus' authority over every aspect of our life. When we surrender to Jesus, the song in our heart ought to be, "Take me, mold me, and make me."

The struggle of living under Jesus' authority is that our sinful nature continues to tempt us to go our own way. We can quickly revert back to desiring to call the shots and tell Jesus how we think we should live. Sometimes we need to be reminded that we have been called to live for God as opposed to God living for us.

Thankfully, God is big enough to handle our pride. Like a good Father, God does not merely see us as his children— God sees the potential in us and longs for us to improve in every area of our life. Taking a step back and examining all of the components of our lives will require intentionality.

In the letter to the church in Thyatira, Jesus helped his church reexamine their core values and inspired them to move out of Mediocreville:

> "Write this letter to the angel of the church in Thyatira. This is the message from the Son of God, whose eyes are like flames of fire, whose feet are like polished bronze:
>
> "I know all the things you do. I have seen your love, your faith, your service, and your patient endurance. And I can see your constant improvement in all these things.

"But I have this complaint against you. You are permitting that woman—that Jezebel who calls herself a prophet—to lead my servants astray. She teaches them to commit sexual sin and to eat food offered to idols. I gave her time to repent, but she does not want to turn away from her immorality.

"Therefore, I will throw her on a bed of suffering, and those who commit adultery with her will suffer greatly unless they repent and turn away from her evil deeds. I will strike her children dead. Then all the churches will know that I am the one who searches out the thoughts and intentions of every person. And I will give to each of you whatever you deserve.

"But I also have a message for the rest of you in Thyatira who have not followed this false teaching ('deeper truths,' as they call them—depths of Satan, actually). I will ask nothing more of you except that you hold tightly to what you have until I come. To all who are victorious, who obey me to the very end,

To them I will give authority over all the nations.
They will rule the nations with an iron rod
    and smash them like clay pots.

"They will have the same authority I received from my Father, and I will also give them the morning star!

"Anyone with ears to hear must listen to the Spirit and understand what he is saying to the churches." (Rev. 2:18–29 NLT)

Thyatira 101

If the Ephesian Christians were tempted by lovelessness, Smyrnean Christians by persecution, and Pergamum's Christians by compromised teachings, then economic pressures seem to have been the primary source of temptation for Thyatira's Christians.

The city of Thyatira was located on a major trade route from the Mediterranean Sea to the East. Thyatira benefited from the trade traffic flowing both ways. Its location also gave people easy access to the markets of the Roman world. Within the city, there were many industrial businesses such as bronze workers, coppersmiths, metal workers, tanners, dyers, potters, and bakers. Most of these crafty professions were managed through a trade guild.[1]

Ancient trade guilds were powerful associations of producers that trained craftspeople, maintained control over production, regulated competition and prices, and restricted the entry of new people into the trade. They had been granted the monopoly right to produce and trade in specific products by the rulers of the land.

Those who did not participate in this aspect of public economic life would risk a substantial measure of their livelihood by refusing to join trade guilds. The guild meetings included a common meal dedication to the guild's patron deity—a meal which would be considered off-limits to more conventional Christians (see Acts 15:20; 1 Cor. 10:19–22). This dynamic within the business community created a severe tension for Christian tradespeople. Not participating in the guild might mean limited business opportunities, but engaging in the guild would certainly require a Christian to compromise his or her beliefs and discipleship to Jesus.

Interestingly, most historians acknowledge the Christian fish symbol (*ichthys*) emerged during the first century. When threatened by the rulers of the land, Christians used the fish symbol to subtly mark meeting places and tombs, or to distinguish friends from foes.[2]

When a disciple of Jesus would cross paths with someone along the road or in the marketplace who was a potential believer, the individual would draw the upper half of the fish symbol on the ground.

If the other person recognized the symbol, the stranger would add a second curved line and complete the fish image.

This fish symbol was a very simple shape to draw. It could be drawn quickly and erased just as fast if there was no sign of recognition on the part of the stranger. Historians acknowledge this secret symbol could have been one of the ways Christian tradespeople related with one another.

In addition to the economic pressures, there were also many different Greek deities who held centers of worship in Thyatira. One of the major deities was Apollo, the sun-god. It's interesting to note, Apollo was later equated with the Roman emperor and they were both worshiped as the sons of Zeus.[3]

In Revelation 2:18 (NLT), the phrase "Son of God" is strategically used as a reference to Jesus. This is the only place in Revelation where this title is used. Along with having the title Son of God, the characteristics of eyes "like flames of fire" and feet "like polished bronze" would have immediately set Jesus in stark contrast to Apollo, the bright, radiant, sun-like god who was also the son of a pagan god, Zeus.[4] Apollo's link with Helios, the sun god, could have also amplified the contrast implicit in Jesus' fiery features.[5]

The disciples in Thyatira were praised by Jesus because they were willing to continually improve and grow as his disciples. Jesus acknowledged they were doing the right things. They were loving, faithful, and willing to serve, all the while, enduring tempting and difficult situations. In everything they were improving.

However, there was one area in which they struggled. Again, we see a church community accommodating false teachings, blending the secular culture with Christ, and this reality made Jesus very disappointed.

Like Balaam, the false prophet in Pergamum, the false prophetess of Thyatira receives the nickname of "Jezebel" (v. 20). Jesus' title for this prophetess immediately calls to mind multiple associations.

Around the year 860 BC, the biblical Jezebel was the idolatrous queen of Israel who introduced the worship of Baal, a pagan idol.[6] Jezebel was not necessarily a prophetess but she sponsored 850 false prophets (1 Kings 18:19), and she sought to take the lives of God's true prophets (1 Kings 18:13; 19:2).[7] Within the biblical record, Jezebel goes down in history as a shameful leader who led God's people astray.

The main problem with the church in Thyatira was the fact that they permitted this Jezebel-like false prophetess to continue teaching the people. The church in Pergamum may have passively accommodated false teachers, but in Thyatira, it seems as if they were fully accepting of the false teachings.

As always, Jesus is very willing to give people their space and allow individuals a period of time where they can process necessary discipleship changes. However, there comes a time when the clock runs out and if a person is doing more harm than good by having their space, then they must be removed from influential leadership. In the Thyatira situation, the Jezebel-like woman was influencing others in two big no-no areas: (1) sexual sin and (2) eating food sacrificed to pagan idols.

Jesus used multiple images to communicate the severity of conforming to the patterns of this world. Jesus declared the woman will be cast upon a "bed of suffering," which is most likely an image of her experiencing the consequences of living outside of God's favor and will. Furthermore, those who were being influenced by this woman and committed adultery with her were also informed they would "suffer intensely" (Rev. 2:22).

Apparently, personal suffering was not enough. Jesus wanted his true disciples to know the woman's children (likely her disciples in her house churches) would also be affected by her lifestyle decisions. The reference to Jesus striking the woman's children or disciples down in death (v. 23) ought to be taken spiritually, not literally. It is likely the woman's disciples had found Christ and had gone from death to life, but if she continued down the path of sin, then she would inevitably take her disciples back into the fallen world of the spiritually dead.

It is also interesting to note that Jesus has the power to discern people's intentions and inner motivations. Revelation 2:23 tunes us into the real problem within the church in Thyatira. The problem was not just a matter of external conformity—it was an internal attitude.

Jesus always prioritizes being before doing. Disciples of Jesus should be trying to figure out Who Would Jesus Be (WWJB) before they consider What Would Jesus Do (WWJD).

Peculiarly, some first-century heretical groups, which this Jezebel-like woman may have embraced, held to the teaching that it was an individual's duty to experience every kind of sin. The goal was to allow the fleshly nature to wallow in sin but keep the soul unaffected. It is highly probable that those who knew the "so-called deep secrets" (v. 24), or "deeper truths . . . depths of Satan" (v. 24 NLT), were those who were deliberately plumbing evil to its depths and still claiming to be pure before God.

To all the rest who weren't believing "Satan's so-called deep secrets," Jesus made one simple request: "hold on to what you have until I come" (vv. 24–25). Those who are victorious and obey everything Jesus commanded will be given authority over the nations and the gift of the Morning Star, who is Jesus himself (vv. 26–28). The promises to the conquerors indicate they have become like Christ in the world, and they have his authority and presence with them everywhere they go.

Catalytic Grace

One of the most freeing things we can experience in God's kingdom is heaps of grace. Grace is realizing God is for us, not against us. However, God's grace is not a cop-out for not doing what God wants us to do. One of the discipleship lessons which was so freeing to me, when I finally returned to Jesus, was beginning to realize God's grace was designed to catapult me forward into places of truth. As Romans 2:4 declares: God's kindness leads us toward repentance.

As I was growing up in my church, I was made to feel if I was not perfect then God was going to give me a swat to hell. Failing in my walk with God or being caught in disobedience felt like being disciplined by my principal. I was unaware of a kind and forgiving God. I only knew of a God who had the power to deliver consequences.

It was a huge relief to discover God is not solely a disciplinarian. God simply wants the best for my life. As I began to view God as kind and loving, I also noticed my motivation for conquering temptation and pursuing God's best began to radically change. I did not just want to avoid being punished, I longed to continually grow and live in God's truth.

It's helpful to know the word *disciple* means one who is a continual learner. By definition, a disciple is a work in progress.

As noted in the letter to the church in Thyatira, Jesus is willing to give his followers space to process the cost of discipleship. Although, just like with any relationship, there are boundaries and appropriate time limits set on that space.

I like to think of it this way: come just as you are, but don't stay that way! Jesus offers us grace and space in order to allow us to grow and learn within our natural rhythms of life, but we ought not take Jesus' generosity for granted.

Within the letter to the church in Thyatira, there is also a warning to every church of every age. A church which is filled with people does not necessarily mean it is a church filled with genuine disciples. It is possible for a church to be overflowing with people because they have come to be entertained instead of instructed, and to be massaged instead of messaged with the reality of sin and the offer of a life-changing salvation.

Saint Bernard of Clairvaux once said, "Hell is full of good intentions." A herd of good-intentioned observers does not automatically please Jesus, but a group of intentional continual learners does. Committed disciples of Jesus must make the shift from having good intentions to being intentional. Intentionality is what takes us down the road of improvement.

Smashing Clay Pots

One of the great temptations for Christ-followers is to consume knowledge and crave spiritual experiences without transforming those insights and events into intentional movement forward.

It saddens my heart to hear about other religious movements, which do not believe in the death and resurrection of Jesus Christ, that are spreading at rapid rates. Yet, Christian churches are struggling to plant more churches than they are closing. I suspect there is a direct link to the fact that many disciples of Christ have become passive and inactive in their faith.

Many church leaders have begun proposing this question to their church communities: If we closed our doors today, would anyone notice or care? However, we also need to make it personal and ask the question: If I moved away from my community, would anyone notice or care?

At the end of the letter to Thyatira, Jesus stated:

> To all who are victorious, *who obey me to the very end*, to them I will give authority over all the nations. They will rule the nations with an iron rod and smash them

like clay pots. They will have the same authority I received from my Father, and I will also give them the morning star! (Rev. 2:26–28 NLT, emphasis added)

Without a doubt, our obedience isn't designed to have us sitting on the bench. Our obedience is designed to allow God to work in us and do something remarkable in the world—with the same authority as Jesus!

Intentional Evaluation

If we truly want to improve and become more intentional in our relationship with God, then we need to take time to evaluate the factors leading us toward personal revival.

Here are seven important evaluative questions:

1. Every moment is a new opportunity to live in God's peace and presence. Are you making the most of every moment?
2. Consider the environments you are living in. The right relationships will lead you in the right direction. The wrong relationships will lead you in the wrong direction. Are your relationships leading you in the right direction?
3. Know who you are and how God wired you. Get a strong handle on your passions, spiritual gifts, and

weaknesses. Are you using your gifts to fulfill your purposes or God's purposes in the world?

4. Choose to live with purpose. Identify what God is calling you to contribute toward his mission on earth. At your funeral, what do you want people to say was your greatest contribution?

5. Planning and strategizing will allow God to shape your path. Even though we must always be paying attention to God's audibles, do you live with a sense of clear direction and calling?

6. We live in a world of constant distraction, with all kinds of things begging for our attention. Are you consistently turning off the disruptions and listening for God's voice?

7. Successful people are constantly seeking wisdom and counsel. Do you have people around you that you can ask for godly wisdom and spiritual discernment?

Discussion Questions

- What does it look like to be continually improving in your relationship with God?

- Imagine if Jesus did an evaluation on your life. What areas do you think he would note as in need of improvement?

- Who are the people around you following Christ closely? How might you begin to imitate some of their actions?

- A great step to being intentional about your spiritual growth is to consistently meet with a mentor you look up to. Do you have a regular meeting pattern with a mentor/ disciple-maker? If not, how can you begin developing this relationship in your life?

- If we are going to be intentional in our spiritual growth, then we need to have goals. What are your yearly, monthly, weekly, and daily spiritual-growth goals?

5 | Sardis

Alive and Alarmed

> *Many do not recognize the fact as they ought, that Satan has got men fast asleep in sin and that it is his great device to keep them so. He does not care what we do if he can do that. We may sing songs about the sweet by and by, preach sermons and say prayers until doomsday, and he will never concern himself about us, if we don't wake anybody up. But if we awake the sleeping sinner, he will gnash on us with his teeth. This is our work—to wake people up.*
> —Catherine Booth

B eep, beep, beep, beep, beep, beep, beep, beep, beep, beep, beep, beep . . .

If there is one noise that I dread the most, it is the irritating sound of an alarm clock.

When I was in college, I had a terrible time waking up, which resulted in regularly being late for class. I was incredibly skilled at hitting the snooze button. At one point, I wised up and decided to place my alarm clock across the room. My idea almost worked, except my roommates weren't very happy because I could sleep right through the beeps.

Even though I am not a big fan of waking up, I am thankful I hear my annoying alarm clock every morning. The irritating beep reminds me I am still alive and have been granted another day to live in the kingdom of God.

For various reasons, the church in Sardis looked like a sleepy dorm room to Jesus. In the letter to the Sardines, Jesus presents himself as the irritating alarm.

Beep, beep, beep, beep, beep, beep, beep . . .

It is time to wake up disciples! Here is the letter to the church in Sardis:

> "Write this letter to the angel of the church in Sardis. This is the message from the one who has the seven-fold Spirit of God and the seven stars:
>
> "I know all the things you do, and that you have a reputation for being alive—but you are dead. Wake up! Strengthen what little remains, for even what is left is almost dead. I find that your actions do not meet the requirements of my God. Go back to what you heard and believed at first; hold to it firmly. Repent and turn

to me again. If you don't wake up, I will come to you suddenly, as unexpected as a thief.

"Yet there are some in the church in Sardis who have not soiled their clothes with evil. They will walk with me in white, for they are worthy. All who are victorious will be clothed in white. I will never erase their names from the Book of Life, but I will announce before my Father and his angels that they are mine.

"Anyone with ears to hear must listen to the Spirit and understand what he is saying to the churches." (Rev. 3:1–6 NLT)

Sardis 101

The history of the city of Sardis is quite fascinating. In 547 BC, Sardis was the site of one of the major battles of history. Sardis was a very wealthy city and it was a major economic and political center in Asia, which made it quite desirable by other rulers.

Sardis had an incredible fortress around the city, but twice in its history, Sardis became so complacent about its fortitude that they were captured by the enemy. During King Cyprus's expansion of Persian control, Sardis fell when Cyprus sent a man to climb a narrow crevice into the sleeping city and open the gates for the invading army. In 218 BC, Antiochus repeated the same performance when he sent fifteen men up the wall to open the gates, again, while the city slept.[1]

It seems the city of Sardis liked to hit the snooze button!

As a place of economic power, Sardis was also filled with the trappings of the Roman religious world. It possessed a large Temple of Artemis, which had been identified with the worship of Cybele, a local goddess. Cybele was the patron deity of Sardis and was believed to have had the power to restore the dead to life.[2] This insight is a unique part of Jesus' imagery. Jesus is contrasting himself with Cybele. The one true God raised Jesus from the dead, and through him, everyone can go from death to life (Eph. 2:6).

At the beginning of the letter, Jesus also described himself as the one who has the "sevenfold Spirit of God and the seven stars" (Rev. 3:1a NLT). The number seven is the Jewish number of fullness or completeness, and the reference to the seven stars may be a description of Jesus looking down upon the church, because he mentioned how he knew about everything they were doing—or were not doing, in this case—(v. 1b).

Clearly, Sardis is the first of the really bad churches. Other than mentioning that there are a few who have not defiled themselves (v. 4), the letter to the disciples in Sardis is a pretty potent rebuke and plea for repentance.

Like the history of Sardis, Jesus described the church as asleep and commanded them to "Wake up!" (v. 2). The disciples were not fulfilling their commitment to follow and obey Jesus' commands, causing them to miss out on God's best for their lives.

The image of the undefiled or unsoiled garment also plays an important role in the overarching message of the letter. In the Roman world, and in the Jewish culture, a person's clothing was a representation of who a person was or what position he or she held in the society. For example, in Genesis 35:2, when Jacob attempted to purify his family, he ordered them to put away their foreign gods and change their clothes. The apostle Paul also picks up on this clothing metaphor and tells the church in Rome to "clothe yourselves with the Lord Jesus Christ, and do not think about how to gratify the desires of the flesh" (Rom. 13:14).

In the letter to the church in Sardis, Jesus used the image of putting on white clothing as a symbol so they would stand out from the surrounding culture and remain pure in his eyes (Rev. 3:4). Interestingly, throughout the pagan temples in Asia and elsewhere, worshipers dared not approach deities with soiled clothes. The normal clothes for approaching the gods in the temples was white or linen.[3]

Jesus presumably promises here that his true followers, who have not polluted themselves with the paganism of their culture, will participate in the good life found in "the new Jerusalem" (Rev. 21:1–2), a wall-less spiritual city filled with the presence of God (v. 22).

The implications for the church in Sardis are clear. It is asleep. It is worthless, and it will eventually be conquered by the evil one if it does not change.

However, for those who were willing to live victoriously and stay pure in the eyes of God, Jesus promised to place their names in God's book, "the book of life" (Rev. 3:5).

Names in the ancient world were not just a practicality, they were an identification of a person's nature and being. When people spoke of doing something in the name of (fill in the blank), they were describing doing something in the essence of another, more powerful being.

Jesus also promises that God's faithful people would not be blotted out from God's Book of Life (v. 5). The image of blotting out stems from Exodus 32:32–33, which came to be applied to a heavenly Book of Life (also mentioned in Ps. 69:28 and Luke 10:20). John's audience in the first century may have heard this image against the citizenship registry known throughout Asia Minor. In some places (best documented from Athens), names of fallen citizens were deleted from the registry immediately prior to their execution.[4]

As already discussed, a central theme throughout Revelation is having a new name and new nature. The new name is not another surname or nickname—it is the name of Jesus. When Jesus said he will "acknowledge that name before my Father" (Rev. 3:5), he is affirming his own name and nature operating within the person.

In a very real way, Christians were meant to be little Christs.

Autopilot

Have you ever wondered: *Where did the time go?* Have you ever made it to the end of the week and wondered what you have accomplished?

Life can become busy, and time can pass by so quickly. Hours, days, months, seasons, and years seem to slip right by. Sometimes we might feel like we are simply on autopilot, going through life without purpose or a sense of accomplishment.

The church in Sardis needed to hear the alarming voice of Jesus so they would rise again and fill themselves with eternal purpose and meaning. They were swiftly falling into the slumber of doing their Christian duties and routines without their heart experiencing continual transformation.

From Jesus' view, the church in Sardis looked like canned sardines. The church had become lifeless instead of life-giving, and they needed to see Jesus afresh.

Seeing Jesus

The New Testament is filled with many stories of people seeing Jesus after his resurrection. Many scholars point to these sightings as evidence of something supernatural happening to Jesus' body.

Somehow, Jesus was alive—again.

In the age of Jesus, people were not absent-minded toward the laws of nature. The ancient and first-century worlds were determined that dead people cannot be resurrected. Even the Jewish people, who did believe in a final resurrection at the end of time for all those who trusted and obeyed God, did not believe anyone had risen from the dead or would do so before the final resurrection.[5]

So, when Jesus was described as *raised from the dead,* what would this have meant in the first-century world? And what did the disciples see when Jesus appeared to them?

In the first century, resurrection was typically used to describe an event which would occur sometime after death, but was not a reference to the state which people went to immediately after death. Most people knew about ghostly beings, unseen spirits, and extrasensory visions, but the concept of resurrection had little to do with the spiritual world. Resurrection specifically referred to something which happened to a person's physical body.[6]

For this reason, when the first-century world said Jesus had resurrected or they had seen Jesus raised from the dead, they were saying something happened to Jesus' material body. The resurrection of Jesus may have contained some supernatural components, but it certainly cannot be written off as a myth.[7]

It's important to recognize Jesus never denied the Jewish perspective of the final resurrection, but he did add a new component. In Matthew 12:40, Jesus used the analogy of Jonah to describe his resurrection weekend: "For as Jonah was three days and three nights in the belly of a huge fish, so the Son of Man will be three days and three nights in the heart of the earth."

The disciples may have initially misunderstood Jesus, but once they saw Jesus in his risen form, the resurrection began to make perfect sense. To use a cliff-diving metaphor, Jesus was the first to leap into God's new kingdom initiative.

The initial resurrection of Jesus meant it was only a matter of time before every God-follower would be caught up in the second, or final, resurrection and allowed to join him in the perfected kingdom realm.

The early disciples promptly began referring to Jesus as the *firstborn of the dead* (Col. 1:18), and they began to anticipate Jesus' triumphal return to the top of the cliff for the second big leap (a.k.a. the Second Coming).[8]

The first leap of Jesus changed the disciples' entire worldview—especially their perspective of earthly pain and suffering. In cliff-diving, knowing what to expect as you take your leap of faith is half the battle. If cliff-diving trainers can effectively equip their jumpers with the process and model it for them, they will be less likely to chicken out when they are called upon to take their flying leap.

In a similar way, the resurrection could be described as Jesus' training episode, and the disciples were being equipped to transition into the perfected future realm of God. After Jesus' disciples were exposed to the resurrection process, earthly trials would have been considered less of a challenge or, to some, even irrelevant.[9]

This is why the early disciples began to develop a new language for what God was doing on earth. Followers of Christ started referring to themselves as new creations (2 Cor. 5:17). They began to proclaim that, in Jesus, the old nature was gone and the new had come!

The early disciples believed, in a very real way, not only were their personal lives being made new, but the entire world as well. Those who joined the new-creation movement discovered that the construction of God's earthly renewal project—the Holy City—was underway.

Construction

A few years ago, we were preparing for our nephew to live with our family. Our house isn't very big, so I decided to build a room for him in our unfinished basement.

As I began working on the project, Josiah, my then five-year-old, wanted to contribute. As you can imagine, five-year-olds are not all that helpful on a construction site, but I wanted to make sure my boy felt like he was making a contribution. So I allowed him to hold my screws, hand me tools, and pick up little odds and ends.

On one particular evening, I was installing the outlets in the walls and, sure enough, the moment I turned away, Josiah decided to test the live outlet with a pair of pliers. You can probably guess what happened. I will forever feel terrible about that moment; he got zapped pretty good.

It was remarkable, though—after my boy recovered from his shock, he still wanted to help. Nothing was going to hold him back! It's like he was convinced he was needed and, if he didn't contribute, then his cousin might not be able to move in. I respected my son's dedication. I liked the fact that he was willing to continue working even after a 110-volt zap. It's the same with God's vision of life in his kingdom. God does not need watchers; God needs workers who are willing to take a few zaps.

Before Jesus was constructing theology, he was constructing buildings. Since Jesus followed in his father's profession as a construction guy, he often used building images and metaphors to communicate with his audience.

On one occasion, Jesus said to a crowd: "The stone the builders rejected has become the cornerstone" (Matt. 21:42a). In the first century, many buildings were made out of stone, and a good 90-degree cornerstone could set a project into motion.

The stone Jesus was referring to was himself and the builders were the Jewish leaders. The issue wasn't *what* God's people were building; the issue was *who* they were building on. God had given the builders the perfect corner-stone, yet they continued to desire the awkwardly shaped stone. Because of the Jewish leaders' unwillingness to build on Jesus, God was required to accept applications for new kingdom-builders.[10]

The unique thing about God's new kingdom project was everyone who applied and accepted God's special corner-stone was given a job to do. In addition, God's prerequisites for his laborers were not overly complicated. In fact, the only thing they needed before entering the worksite was to be willing to learn.

The early disciples understood that, one day, Jesus would return and God's construction project would be complete. But, in the meantime, every believer must pick up their tools and get to work. Ditching the kingdom work or falling asleep on the job was simply unacceptable.

From time to time, there were a few Christ-followers who started slacking off on the job, but the leaders of the early church were quick to realign their work crews. The author of Hebrews boldly proclaimed:

> We want each of you to show this same diligence to the very end, so that what you hope for may be fully realized. We do not want you to become lazy, but to imitate those who through faith and patience inherit what has been promised. (6:11–12)

The question every disciple needs to be able to answer is: In what ways am I diligently continuing and contributing till the very end?

Renewal

Throughout the book of Revelation, the image of God's renewed world becomes incredibly important, especially for the church in Sardis. John wanted to make sure every disciple in every age understood that God was going to usher in a new heaven and new earth, which began on earth and would continue throughout eternity.

In Revelation 21:2–5a, John said:

> I saw the Holy City, the new Jerusalem, *coming down* out of heaven from God, prepared as a bride beautifully dressed for her husband. And I heard a loud voice from the throne saying, "Look! God's dwelling place is now among the people, and he will dwell with them. They will be his people, and God himself will be with them and be their God. 'He will wipe every tear from their eyes. There will be no more death' or mourning or crying or pain, for the old order of things has passed away."
>
> He who was seated on the throne said, "I am making *everything new*!" (emphasis added)

It is important to understand John was not referring to a literal building or city, but to the realm of God which is absent of evil and the rebellious order.[11]

Notice the city is "coming down" out of heaven from God to the earth. Here, John is trying to communicate to the church, the bride of Christ, that God is already in the process of coming down. One day, the project will be complete; but right now, the important thing to know is God is coming from the future into humanity's present.

This new realm which is filled with the presence of God is exactly what God's people are supposed to be living in and offering as a gift to the next generation. This new reality is not something they are waiting to experience one day in the future—it is something they are experiencing right now.

In Revelation 21:14–17, John described the dimensions of this spiritual city:

> The wall of the city had twelve foundations, and on them were the names of the twelve apostles of the Lamb.
>
> The angel who talked with me had a measuring rod of gold to measure the city, its gates and its walls. The city was laid out like a square, as long as it was wide. He measured the city with the rod and found it to be 12,000 stadia in length, and as wide and high as it is long. The angel measured the wall using human measurement, and it was 144 cubits thick.

The wall of the city had twelve foundations, which John tells us right away are the twelve apostles of Jesus. John goes on to mention the city was laid out like a square. We know within the center of the Jewish temple there was a room called the Holy of Holies, which was also laid out in a square and was considered to be the dwelling place of God's presence. However, in this passage, John is describing a new type of temple—a temple of the Holy Spirit (1 Cor. 6:19–20).

Another feature to the cubic city was its size. John says it measured "12,000 stadia in length," which would be about 1,400 miles.

This is a fascinating image of a map of the Roman Empire within the first century. If you were to place a 1,400-mile cubic city around the Island of Patmos, where John was writing from, the cubic city would encompass all of the known church communities at the time Revelation was written.[12]

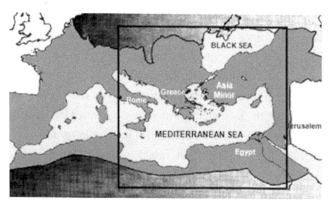

John's vision reveals how the New Jerusalem—the new center of worship, which is coming down from God—is the bride of Christ, the church's presence on earth. The people of God are now the epicenter of God's presence and the newly founded clusters of churches are the work camps for God's missional endeavors.

Without a doubt, the church is God's strategic vision of hope for the world. If you were a persecuted Christian living in the first century, then the revelation of this New Jerusalem meant all the pain and suffering for Christ was worth it, precisely because God was in the process of making all things new. The church, the body of Christ, was not just a nice accessory to life—it was a lifeline and the primary means for unleashing the healing presence of God into the world.

The reason the early disciples, and the "few" disciples in Sardis (Rev. 3:4), should be able to endure hardship, persecution, and even death was because they believed God's kingdom project was not finished, but in the works.

I have some friends who just finished building their house. A few years ago, they bought their property, erected a barn, and began working on their home. For months they lived out of their barn while they labored on the house. I was never able to understand how they functioned as a family, but I suspect the only reason they were able to do so was because they had hope that, one day soon, they would find themselves living inside their dream home.

You see, when we know God's heavenly kingdom is already being built on earth and God is already in the process of making our dream home, it makes it entirely possible to overcome every temptation and remain alive in Christ.

One day God's eternal project will be fully completed, but until then, we must be content to live in the barn and work toward its completion.

How Does Your Life Read?

You've probably heard the old English idiom: "Don't judge a book by its cover." Sometimes a book can have an awful-looking cover, but inside it is incredibly awe-inspiring. Other times, a book can have a slick cover, but the content feels like a walk through a sludge-filled swamp.

In a sense, Jesus was trying to convey to his disciples in Sardis that their life-cover was not what really mattered. What should matter most is the Jesus-like content on the inside. Thankfully, Jesus does not judge us by our cover; he judges us by our content.

Jesus' message to the church in Sardis reminds us that we cannot fake God out and we cannot fake out those who are peering into our lives. When Jesus begins to sense we are faking it, he hits the alarm!

Truth be told, if the movement of God is going to continue to expand on earth, every disciple of Jesus needs to hear Jesus' alarm sound off. We must arise and find our God-designed destiny. We cannot afford to sleep in, continually hitting the snooze button on life with God.

God desires for us to immerse ourselves in his mission in the world. No matter where we are at in the journey of life, we must know it is never too late. Whether we are twelve or eighty-two, we must arise, go for God, and live like every moment matters.

Jesus is calling all his disciples into a new opportunity. It is never too late for a revival of the heart.

Discussion Questions

- On a scale from 1–10, how alive are you in Christ?

- Is there anything you are doing that could be replaced with something else that brings a contribution to God's kingdom? If so, are you willing to replace it?

- How much does prayer and Scripture study impact your everyday decision-making?

- Has God placed a vision for your life on your heart that you have ignored or neglected? What would happen in your life if you accepted your call and made a kingdom difference?

6 | Philadelphia

Persevering and Passionate

> *Gospel truth seeks no corners,*
> *because it fears no trials.*
> —Matthew Henry

Before you read this chapter, go online and view this must-see video clip: www. vimeo.com/25249737.

This 1992 Olympic moment has been heralded as one of the most motivational memories in the history of sports. There are many dynamics involved in the story line, which make it extremely moving and a real tear-jerker.

If the moment when Derek Redmond springs back onto his feet after he tore his hamstring doesn't tug on your heartstrings, then the image of his father rushing out to help him cross the finish line certainly will. I get choked up every time I watch the clip because of the father's love. In many ways, it reminds me of my heavenly Father's love.

It is evident from the video clip that Redmond was committed to finishing the race and he was not about to give up. He was willing to persevere even when his body was severed. This kind of per[sever]ance does not just take verbal commitment—it takes unbridled passion.

Late in his life, the apostle Paul, who knew a thing or two about perseverance and passion, wrote these words to his protégé: "I have fought the good fight, I have finished the race, and I have remained faithful" (2 Tim. 4:7 NLT).

Passion and perseverance go hand in hand. Together they run.

The next letter we are going to explore was written to the church in Philadelphia. In the letter, we will discover some characteristics of discipleship which have gone missing in the modern church era. Let's enter into Philadelphia and find out what it takes to finish well:

> "Write this letter to the angel of the church in Philadelphia.
>
> This is the message from the one who is holy and true,
>   the one who has the key of David.
> What he opens, no one can close;
>   and what he closes, no one can open:

"I know all the things you do, and I have opened a door for you that no one can close. You have little strength, yet you obeyed my word and did not deny me. Look, I will force those who belong to Satan's synagogue—those liars who say they are Jews but are not—to come and bow down at your feet. They will acknowledge that you are the ones I love.

"Because you have obeyed my command to persevere, I will protect you from the great time of testing that will come upon the whole world to test those who belong to this world. I am coming soon. Hold on to what you have, so that no one will take away your crown. All who are victorious will become pillars in the Temple of my God, and they will never have to leave it. And I will write on them the name of my God, and they will be citizens in the city of my God—the new Jerusalem that comes down from heaven from my God. And I will also write on them my new name.

"Anyone with ears to hear must listen to the Spirit and understand what he is saying to the churches." (Rev. 3:7–13 NLT)

Philadelphia 101

The city of Philadelphia was a relatively new city in the first century. *Philadelophos* is the Greek word for one who loves his brother, or brotherly love. Philadelphia was founded with the deliberate intention to be a missionary of Greek culture to the surrounding regions of Lydia and Phrygia. The experiment worked. By AD 19, the Lydians had forgotten their own language and were thoroughly Greek.[1]

In the letter, Jesus commented on how he knows the things they do (Rev. 3:8 NLT). Presumably, the deeds Jesus saw were the good deeds, which were transforming the culture around them. Jesus was subtly reminding his faithful followers that, just as the city of Philadelphia was also given an open door to spread Greek ideas throughout the region, the church in Philadelphia was given an open door to spread the word of God. The church in Philadelphia was founded with the deliberate intention of being missionaries in the land, offering a fresh palate of Jesus' culture.

The description of Jesus being "holy and true, who holds the key of David" is also an important image to grasp (v. 7). The key of David is a symbol of authority. Behind this idea is an Old Testament narrative. In Isaiah 22:22, the prophet Isaiah heard God say of his faithful steward Eliakim: "And I will place on his shoulder the *key* to the house of David; what he opens no one can shut, and what he shuts no one can open." It is clear all throughout Revelation, Jesus alone has the key to the kingdom, and he has the authority over all of the citizens of God's Holy City on earth. Jesus is understood as the one who determines who may enter his household and who may not.[2]

This Davidic imagery may have been utilized by Jesus because of the strong opposition, which was coming from the Jewish synagogue, referenced as "Satan's synagogue" in the letter (Rev. 3:9 NLT). King David was the great king of the Jews, and it was believed that the Jewish Messiah would come as one like David.[3] Ironically, the Jewish clan, who did not accept Jesus as the world's Messiah, went on to be one of the primary persecutors of the early church.

As in Smyrna, believers in Philadelphia experienced conflict with the local Jewish synagogues. The situation between the Jewish and Christian communities was quite complicated. The Jewish people were permitted by Rome to remain thoroughly Jewish as long as they did not stir up any trouble. To Rome, the early Christians were looked upon as a Jewish subset, yet the Christians were attracting and converting many Gentiles (non-Jewish people). This dynamic could have caused Rome to question the motives of the Jews, and potentially lose them their privileged status with Rome. Because of this, the Jewish communities excommunicated the early Christians and expelled them from their houses of worship.[4]

With this relational strain in mind, it makes sense for Jesus to use the language of "the synagogue of Satan" (v. 9).[5] Even though the Christians were pushed out of the synagogue, Jesus is seen as the one who would welcome the outcast believers into his own household and kingdom reign on earth, "the new Jerusalem" (Rev. 3:12; 21:2).

It is not a coincidence that one of the major themes of this letter happens to be perseverance. The city of Philadelphia was known as the city of comebacks. Philadelphia was located on the edge of a great plain called Katakekaumene, which means burnt land.

The Katakekaumene was a great volcanic plain bearing the marks of lava and ashes from the volcanoes. As it turns out, this type of land is extremely fertile. The region ended up becoming famous for grape-growing and became the center for the worship of Dionysus, the god of wine.[6]

In addition to the volcanoes, another cataclysmic event, an earthquake, occurred in AD 17. The earthquake destroyed Philadelphia, Sardis, and many other cities in the region. The post-quake tremors went on for many years.

Often, countries which are demolished by earthquakes will rise up and rebuild with confidence. However, the constant tremors kept the city in panic mode and, as a result, the city became a ghost town. Most of the population lived in so much fear they moved to the outskirts of the city and lived in makeshift huts.[7] Yet, there were a few people in the city who were willing to persevere through the tremors and risk their lives against the falling masonry. Those who still dared to live in the city spent their time fixing up the build-ings, with the hopes of redeeming the city.

Even more, the city of Philadelphia knew what it was like to receive a new name, which is a metaphor Jesus stra-tegically inserted into his message. When the earthquake struck, Caesar Tiberius was generous toward the city and helped fund the rebuilding project. As a result, the city changed its name to Neocaesarea (the New City of Caesar). Shortly after the name change, when Caesar Vespasian was ruler, the city once again changed its name to Flavia, which was Vespasian's family name. Neither of the name changes lasted, but the city of Philadelphia became very aware of the dynamics involved in receiving a new name and identity.[8]

Toward the end of the letter, Jesus associated Philadelphia's name and identity shifts and declared that his followers who persevered to the end would receive a new name and they would be considered citizens of God's Holy City, "the new Jerusalem," which had come down out of heaven to earth (Rev. 3:12).

Broken, Not Busted

The church in Philadelphia knew all too well about being persecuted and forced to the outskirts of society. This might be the reason Jesus spent a considerable amount of energy encouraging his disciples. Because of persecution from the Jewish and Greek communities, the church was found to be powerless and weak. Yet the faithful in Philadelphia did not deny Jesus. They were willing to persevere in the face of adversity.

This is also a good reminder of how success in Jesus' eyes is not necessarily a church with power and prosperity. The church in Philadelphia was barely able to hold their lives together; however, Jesus held them in the highest esteem. The church was truly living out the principle the apostle Paul presented in 2 Corinthians 12:9—rejoicing in their weaknesses, since "[God's] power is made perfect in weakness."

The strength of their weakness was how they had obeyed Jesus' commands and remained faithful to Jesus amid great opposition. They did not loosen their commitment to Jesus. They did not take the easier route of becoming an invisible or silent Christian and, because of this, they were able to experience the rich rewards of perseverance.

In Revelation 3:10–13, Jesus declared he would protect his disciples, be present with them, bring peace to them, proclaim them as his, and make them "pillars" in God's holy temple, which is coming down out of heaven to earth.

The image of pillars is a continuation of Jesus' concept of the New Jerusalem used throughout Revelation. Most ancient temples throughout Asia Minor were upheld by pillars, bringing about an awe-inspiring attractiveness to the exterior frontage of the temple. It was also quite common for these pillars to bear honorary inscriptions to gods or goddesses.[9]

Even though God's temple was in the spiritual and unseen realm, it was important for Jesus to recognize the essential role of his followers holding up God's temple for all to experience the awe-inspiring glory of God.

Jesus also mentioned he will "write . . . the name of my God" on his faithful pillars (v. 12). With a great sense of eternal hope, those who persevere to the end will have God's name branded on them and will be considered citizens of God's Holy City.

The naming of the faithful directs us to the deepest of all the dimensions in the death and resurrection of Jesus. Receiving a new name means the faithful have received a new identity. No longer do they need to revel in their old nature and identity; they can live victoriously in their new nature and identity, which is in Christ Jesus!

The Struggle Is Real

Throughout my life, perseverance and passion have always been a struggle. I am a pretty dedicated person—when things are going my way. However, if I am being honest, when things are not giving me a favorable outcome, I struggle to stay committed.

There is a popular locker room saying that goes: "When the going gets tough, the tough get going!" Yet, when I look back on the patterns of my life, I can see many times when I may have started something with fiery vigor, but my passion and dedication waned as soon as it became too difficult or a drag.

Starting and stopping may have been a pattern for most of my life; however, something changed in me soon after I made a commitment to follow Jesus and serve God's mission. In a unique way, God almost instantaneously began to redeem my past patterns and I received a new desire to live a more disciplined life. I discovered the radical truth found in 2 Corinthians 5:17: "Therefore, if anyone is in Christ, the new creation has come: The old has gone, the new is here!"

I cannot say it is always easier to persevere through life's challenges because of following Jesus, but I have experienced a new desire to stick things out and enjoy the refinement of the fire.

"Passionerance"

Much like the persevering dynamics within the first-century city of Philadelphia, Jesus is also calling his twenty-first-century disciples to remain 100-percent committed and passionate to dwelling in God's Holy City on earth.

We might do well to think of our commitment to following Jesus as a 50/50 deal. It takes 50 percent perseverance and 50 percent passion. Perseverance and passion work hand in hand.

We desperately need "passionerance" if we are going to experience personal revival. Passionerance means more than enduring, more than simply holding on. It is a recognition of the fact that our lives are in the hands of God like a bow and arrow in the hands of an archer. God is aiming at our destiny, but we can't always see the target. We may feel more confused than ever while the string tightens down, yet God knows what he is doing and lets the arrow fly. This is the moment of trust and dependence on God. Sometimes we just need to proclaim as Job did: "Though he slay me, yet will I hope in him" (13:15a).

The pillars in Philadelphia knew that faith is not a weak, disjointed emotion, but it is a strong confidence in God's purposes and promises. Even when disaster occurs in our life and we lack willpower, we can still throw ourselves into a total confidence upon God and his eternal purposes. When we do this, we can experience God's hope in any situation. It is this type of complete abandonment to God that catches the attention of the lost world and inspires others to consider our source of strength.

Discussion Questions

- When was the last time you were required to persevere through a difficult situation? What did you learn about dependency on God?

- What things in life are you passionate about? What would happen in your life if you were as passionate about following the way of Jesus as you were about other things?

- How do the concepts of denying yourself and having perseverance relate?

- What has God set in your heart that you know you must do something about?

7 | Laodicea
Rich and Radical

> *When a man becomes a Christian, he becomes*
> *industrious, trustworthy and prosperous. Now, if*
> *that man when he gets all he can and saves all he*
> *can, does not give all he can, I have more hope for*
> *Judas Iscariot than for that man!*
> —John Wesley

How rich are you?

I suspect most of us would say, "Not very!"

When we compare ourselves to people like Warren Buffet, LeBron James, Bill Gates, and Oprah Winfrey, we might feel poor. However, when we compare ourselves to the rest of the world, we would probably look filthy rich.

Money does make the world go 'round, but it can also ground us from experiencing the fullness of God's kingdom on earth.

Recently, my daughter, Jennah, brought my wallet and my heart out into the open. Somewhere in the middle of a bedtime prayer, I had asked God to open our hearts to serve people in need. Immediately after my prayer, Jennah asked me a jaw-dropping question: "Daddy, why don't we do that?"

I inquired further: "Do what?"

"Serve people in need," Jennah replied.

My heart began to cringe and crinkle, realizing I had become an expert at praying for people in need, but being moved into action was absent.

I told Jennah: "I know a guy who has cancer and he is really struggling right now."

"How can we help him?" Jennah asked.

I responded: "I think he really needs money right now because he has a surgery coming up and it is going to be costly."

As Jennah pulled her sheets up, she whispered: "Well, maybe I can give him some of my money in my piggy bank."

"That sounds like a great idea," I remarked.

The prayerful moment with my daughter turned out to be a profound teaching lesson for me. However, I did not expect what I would find the next morning.

As I arose and came down the steps, Jennah was in our living room, stuffing a homemade, uniquely designed envelope with wrinkled-up dollar bills and change.

I asked Jennah what she was doing, and she replied: "I'm giving this money to your friend with cancer."

My heart leaped with joy!

Then I said, "Now, Jennah, you don't have to give everything you have in your piggy bank away."

Ugh.

Seriously, Ed?

What I was really saying was: "Don't be too radical, Jennah. It's nice you wanted to give your hard-earned money away to someone in need, but don't forget about leaving some spending money for you to buy Bubble Tape."

Thankfully, the Spirit quickly nudged my selfish heart. I reframed my attitude and I began to speak blessings and praises over my daughter.

The truth is, Jesus wants radicals to repaint a new picture of richness in the world. For very good reasons, Jesus taught more about money and possessions than he did about any other subject matter.

In one of Jesus' money talks, found in Matthew 6:19–20, Jesus strategically referenced the phrase "treasures in heaven." In the first-century Jewish world, treasure in heaven was not speaking about a treasure chest of gold found in a future heavenly realm. This phrase was a very common Jewish idiom which was used as a reference to a person's character. When Jesus said, "store up for yourselves treasures in heaven," he was referring to our earthly character development.[1]

Jesus knew there was a direct link between a person's character and their perspective on money. Jesus desperately wanted his disciples to move into a radical realm of generosity which would cause the world to stop in their tracks and take notice.

Jesus may have had a ragtag band of disciples, and they may have, more often than not, misunderstood his teachings. However, Jesus knew they were all in. Jesus' Twelve had given up their personal dreams, homes, families, and businesses in order to follow him. They may have had thick skulls, but at least they were willing to give up everything in order to follow Jesus.

Scripture is clear about our salvation not being dependent upon what we do, but it is also very clear God does not want a bunch of partially committed disciples. In many instances, Jesus asked wannabe disciples to give up something close to their heart, including their possessions, before they would be allowed to come and follow him (see Mark 10:21).

The last church on John's list was the church in Laodicea. The Laodiceans needed to hear: "It's time to put your money where your mouth is!" Jesus was tired of their halfway-committed attitudes, so he called them to be radical:

"Write this letter to the angel of the church in Laodicea. This is the message from the one who is the Amen—the faithful and true witness, the beginning of God's new creation:

"I know all the things you do, that you are neither hot nor cold. I wish that you were one or the other! But since you are like lukewarm water, neither hot nor cold, I will spit you out of my mouth! You say, 'I am rich. I have everything I want. I don't need a thing!' And you don't realize that you are wretched and miserable and poor and blind and naked. So I advise you to buy gold from me—gold that has been purified by fire. Then you will be rich. Also buy white garments from me so you will not be shamed by your nakedness, and ointment for your eyes so you will be able to see. I correct and discipline everyone I love. So be diligent and turn from your indifference.

"Look! I stand at the door and knock. If you hear my voice and open the door, I will come in, and we will share a meal together as friends. Those who are victorious will sit with me on my throne, just as I was victorious and sat with my Father on his throne.

"Anyone with ears to hear must listen to the Spirit and understand what he is saying to the churches." (Rev. 3:14–22 NLT)

Laodicea 101

The city of Laodicea was one of the wealthiest cities in the province of Asia. In AD 60 there was an earthquake, which brought great destruction to the city. The Roman government offered rebuilding assistance, but the city of Laodicea refused help from Rome and rebuilt itself in even greater splendor than it previously enjoyed.[2]

Because of Laodicea's location, it was a perfect place for a major banking system. It was also famous for its textile industry, especially the luxurious woolen cloths and rugs made from the special black wool which had been developed through special breeding techniques of black sheep.

In addition to its wealth and manufacturing, Laodicea was the home of a famous medical school associated with the Temple of Men, a Carian god of healing who became associated with Asclepius in Roman times. This school was known especially for its Phrygian powder, from which an ointment was made, effectively curing certain eye diseases.[3] Yet most Laodiceans would also acknowledge the usefulness of divine help alongside their medical establishment. Thus, the city greatly revered both Apollo, the god of prophecy, and Asclepius, the god of healing.[4]

Even though Laodicea had everything and claimed to be self-sufficient, the city lacked one very important thing: good water. The city had no water supply of its own except for what little could be transported from two nearby tributaries of the Lycus River. For utility purposes, water was piped in from the hot springs about six miles away. By the time either water source arrived in Laodicea, the water was lukewarm. The utility water was not used for drinking; however, oddly enough, the innovative healing school in the city required people to cleanse their bodies by drinking the water, which in turn made them vomit.[5]

As with any prosperous Roman city, Laodicea offered the worship of a smorgasbord of Greek gods: Zeus, Dionysus, Helios, Hera, and Athena. Plus, like the other cities John wrote to, Laodicea was also a center of Caesar worship.[6]

In the letter, Jesus powerfully described himself as "the Amen" (Rev. 3:14). In the Hebrew context, the word *amen* was used to signify something true or valid. Jesus seems to be indicating he is the amen to their prayers. He is the true one in the midst of a culture where there are false gods on every corner.[7]

Jesus presented himself and his way as a stark contrast to what the church had become. This is also an insight into the type of disciples the Laodicean church had unknowingly started to produce. The church of Laodicea had become indistinguishable from its surroundings. It was no longer countercultural; it was simply a reflection of the culture. Rather than being a faithful and true witness, like the church in Philadelphia, which might result in persecution or death, the Laodiceans had begun to blend into the culture and operate on the same value system as the fallen world.

As Jesus analyzed the church in Laodicea, the city's water problems and the image of people vomiting from the healing school must have come to mind. Earlier prophets also used images of rotten food to describe God's rejection of people who had grown disgusting to him (see Jer. 24:8), but Jesus contextualizes the image for Laodicean believers.[8] In Revelation 3:16, Jesus essentially declared: "You are just like your water. You are useless. You are just like your surroundings and you make me want to vomit!"

To the Laodicean church, surrounded by the healing center and other luxuries, the imagery of being poor, blind, and naked would have been shockingly confrontational (v. 17).

The disciples in Laodicea were lukewarm. They had adopted the same value system as the culture around them, and as a result, they had become comfortable citizens in a consumeristic culture. The Laodicean type of church fulfills the requirements for the current stream of health-and-wealth, prosperity gospel teaching; however, Jesus named them and claimed them as a church that saddened his heart. To be sure, Christian history is littered with the remains of Laodicean churches. These are the churches that assume the best way to reach a culture is to become like it.

Laodicean-like churches are like the city's water—
useless to Jesus. It might sound harsh, but they might as
well not exist. The world needs to have useful water from
both sides of the faucet. On one side, people need a cool and
refreshing drink of God's love, grace, and forgiveness of sins.
On the other side, they need to see a piping-hot passion for
victims of injustice, poverty, and oppression.

The Laodicean church was not going, was not making
disciples, was not baptizing, and was not teaching everyone
how to obey all of Jesus' commands (see Matt. 28:19–20).
Simply put, the Laodiceans had turned Jesus' Great
Commission into the Great Omission.

Exposed

Even though Jesus was extremely displeased with his disciples in Laodicea, he still expressed his love for them and his
desire to see them repent and return to a countercultural
movement in the land (Rev. 3:19).

Since the Laodicean church was surrounded by immense
wealth, their medical school, and their luxurious black
woolen garments, the imagery of being poor, blind, and
naked would be radically confrontive (Rev. 3:17). Jesus'
alternative vision was for the Laodicean church to come to
him for their needs instead of seeking satisfaction from the

world. In Revelation 3:18, Jesus identifies with the unique identities of Laodicean culture, but counsels the church to, "*Buy from me* gold refined in the fire, so you can become rich; and white cloths to wear, so you can cover your shameful nakedness; and salve to put on your eyes, so you can see."

Because Jesus loved the Laodicean disciples so much, he needed to mention the hard truth that they might have every material possession they could dream of, but they could not see how they were still wretched, miserable, poor, blind, and naked. The church needed to hear how they were falling short of God's best. In a powerful way, Jesus invited the church to reclothe themselves in "white clothes" (v. 18), which is another way of saying being reclothed in the purity of Christ (see Rom. 13:14).

Jesus longs to see his disciples in every era rely solely on him as opposed to relying on their amazing genius and materialistic plenty. If the church was not willing to be transformed from the inside out, Jesus knew they would not be the type of people who would be willing to endure the impending persecution of Rome and praise him through the storms of life.

As soon as the economy crashed, persecution struck, or hardship began to occur, Jesus knew the disciples in Laodicea would not stay faithful and endure. They would most likely be the type of people who follow God when life is good, but as soon as hardships or challenges came their way, they'd bail.

A Friendly Invitation

Like a good friend, Jesus extended an invitation to the church in Laodicea. Jesus painted a picture of himself knocking on the door of their house and heart. If the people were willing to open the door, then Jesus would be willing to step in and share a meal with them (Rev. 3:20).

Here we see Jesus describing the most intimate setting in human relationships, especially within the first-century Jewish context. Eating with someone was a sign of true friendship, which is precisely the type of relationship Jesus wanted with his followers.

Jesus wanted true friends. Friends who will never stab him in the back. Friends who will always come to him in times of need. Friends who will listen to and receive his wisdom for life in God's Holy City.

Happiness or Wholeness

Most of us have grown up in a culture which idolizes fame and wealth. We are hit with hundreds of advertisements and commercials every day; each ad promises to bring us wealth and happiness, making it hard not to consider the sales.

These human desires are precisely what Jesus was warning us about. Jesus said to the church in Laodicea: "You say, 'I am rich. I have everything I want. I don't need a thing!'

And you don't realize you are wretched and miserable and poor and blind and naked" (Rev. 3:17 NLT). This is a good description of modern America, isn't it?

It's quite possible the reason we struggle to remain alive in Christ is because we have pursued everything the world offers to fulfill our needs and wants. However, have you ever felt like you have pursued all the things of this world and are still left wanting—wanting more, that is! The things of this world simply do not bring long-term satisfaction and wholeness.

A friend of mine, who owned a lucrative construction company, once shared his testimony with me. He went on to explain how he spent the majority of his time working in order to keep up with the Joneses. He described how miserable he felt after each major purchase, realizing he was setting himself up to work longer and harder to pay for his stuff. His materialistic hunger was never satisfied until he started following Jesus. In an attempt to follow Jesus more closely, he started to downsize, sell off many of his possessions, and give more to his church's mission. The power in his testimony was when he said, "I can honestly say I am full of life. I finally feel whole. I no longer find satisfaction in having the latest and greatest. I am free—free to be radical for Jesus."

In our world today, there are many examples of radical people. If you don't think so, just turn on the TV! On any given day there are thousands of people at sporting events who are unleashing their radical impulses as they root for their team. These obsessed fans are radical in every way. They cheer like crazy, spend huge amounts of money on the best seats, and even allow the outcome of the game to determine their mood.

Over the years, I have witnessed a lot of radical fans. I have seen people go absolutely bonkers when their team scored a winning point. However, I can't say I've seen a lot of radical Christ-followers. I am not talking about whooping and hollering for Jesus, as if he was the dominant team. I am talking about a sincere enthusiasm and passion for the mission of God on earth.

Imagine if every follower of Jesus were as radical for God's mission on the earth as they are for their favorite sports team. The world might just say: "What's this all about? I've never seen anything like it!"

Discussion Questions

- What do you need to simplify in your life in order to move your riches into the right places so that God can use your riches for his purposes?

- Who are you trying to keep up with or impress?

- Would people around you consider you radical for the cause of Christ?

- If someone looked at your budget, would they consider you radical for the cause of Christ?

- If you were able to do any ministry or mission for God, what would it be? What is stopping you?

Conclusion

Consumed and Concerned

When a Christian shuns fellowship with other Christians, the devil smiles. When one stops studying the Bible, the devil laughs.
     When one stops praying, the devil shouts for joy.
          —Corrie ten Boom

Most of us probably learned a lot about rule-following from our grade school experience. *Stay in line, don't talk when the teacher is talking, and don't be tardy* were all very important rules. However, there was one rule I learned in grade school that changed my life. It is respectfully known as the five-second rule.

The rule states: If someone drops a piece of food on the floor and picks it back up within five seconds, it is still socially acceptable to eat it. If the piece of food lingers on the floor for longer than five seconds, it is tarnished forever and must be thrown away. I was, and still am, a huge fan of the five-second rule.

Don't be thinking: *You're disgusting, Ed. I can't believe you'd do that.* I know you do it, too, especially when no one is looking!

As was stated in the beginning of this book, being a faithful disciple of Jesus and living in his kingdom is not always easy. At some point, we are going to slip up, slide away from Christ, and find ourselves face down in a world of dirt and sin.

Thankfully, our gracious God has a rule. It's not the five-second rule, though. God's rule states: I am always willing to pick you back up and make you useful again.

Snapping the Whip

Without a doubt, remaining alive in Christ and experiencing personal revival will require us to stay connected with a group of encouraging people who are committed to the same kingdom objectives. There is no such thing as a lone disciple. It is nearly impossible to remain a fully devoted disciple of Jesus without someone pushing us forward and without us pulling someone else forward too.

When I was growing up in the '80s, the place to be on Friday night around my hometown was Spinning Wheels roller skating rink. Spinning Wheels had everything a kid needed to be a kid. There was food, friendship, conversation, action, and an occasional secret admirer.

Besides the limbo, my favorite thing to do while skating was a game called snap-the-whip. Snapping-the-whip is when four or five friends lock hands, begin skating, and then as a turn approaches, they fling the person on the end forward at adrenaline-pumping speeds. Even though roller skating had not yet been invented in the first century, snapping-the-whip was precisely what Jesus wanted his followers to do for one another.

In Hebrews 10:22–25, the author wrote:

> So let's do it—full of belief, confident that we're presentable inside and out. Let's keep a firm grip on the promises that keep us going. [God] always keeps his word. Let's see how inventive we can be in encouraging love and helping out, not avoiding worshiping together as some do but spurring each other on, especially as we see the big Day approaching. (The Message)

It doesn't take a rocket scientist to calculate how fast the twenty-first-century church is declining. In a 2019 survey, the Pew Research Center discovered the religiously unaffiliated share of the population, consisting of people who describe their religious identity as atheist, agnostic, or "nothing in particular," now stands at 26 percent, up from 17 percent in 2009.[1]

I suspect most of the people who have left the church would not say they left Jesus, though. For various reasons, they have simply left the structured way of an organized church system.

There's certainly no one-size-fits-all format for connecting with other Christ-followers, but it's important we don't try to snap-the-whip by ourselves. Snapping yourself is kind of awkward-looking. It takes a community of disciple-makers to snap well.

Focus

Within the early church, there was always somebody falling off the bandwagon. The New Testament writers were constantly trying to fix problems, both practically and theologically. Upon a quick observation, it seems like many of the church's issues stemmed from the lack of focus in their overarching goals. The history of the church has proven that when there isn't a clear focal point, inevitably people will focus on their personal preferences, which usually ends up creating quite a mess.

John was observant of this reality, so throughout Revelation, he intentionally placed the spotlight on the focal point: Jesus. In fact, John says at the very beginning of Revelation, this is "the revelation from Jesus Christ" (1:1a). John knew if the church was going to survive and truly create a different world, then the people of God needed to see what they were working toward and how their role affected God's Holy City.

Keep in mind, the community of God's people—the church—is the Holy City, the dwelling place of God on earth. God's Holy City is not a future vision; it is a present reality coming down out of heaven and entering to earth (Rev. 21:2).

In Revelation 21:23–24, John described the Holy City in further detail. John wrote: "The city does not need the sun or the moon to shine on it, for the glory of God gives it light, and the Lamb is its lamp. The nations will walk by its light, and the kings of the earth will bring their splendor into it."

The dynamic aspect of this part of the image is how the Holy City, the church, does not merely receive light (from the sun) or reflect light (from the moon), but it is itself beaming with the light of God's presence.

Jesus described this same reality to his disciples when he said, "You are the light of the world—like a city on a hilltop that cannot be hidden. No one lights a lamp and then puts it under a basket. Instead, a lamp is placed on a stand, where it gives light to everyone in the house. In the same way, let your good deeds shine out for all to see, so that everyone will praise your heavenly Father" (Matt. 5:14–16 NLT).

If we miss this light-giving reality, we will essentially miss out on all of the implications within Jesus' teachings. The radiating light throughout the Holy City is the Lamb (Jesus) and the church is the lampstand.

In the first chapter of Revelation, John tells us how he turned to see the voice who was speaking to him, and he "saw seven gold lampstands" (v. 12). Here, John saw the radiance of both Jesus and the church. The church was the community of people who were holding up and supporting the Light of the world!

Just as John begins his revelation with a powerful image, he also ends it with a grand finale—which should blow our minds if we see it in the proper light.

In chapters 21 and 22, John further describes God's Holy City at work within the midst of human history. John's original hearers would not have been thinking of this image as a future era; they would have realized John was advocating for the church's purpose on earth.

You see, John is exposing us to the reality that the Holy City, the church, has an immense job to do in the world. If this vision is going to be accomplished, then the people of God—whose names are written in God's Book of Life— must come together, encourage one another, and organize for the adrenalin-pumping hope movement.

In recent days, the idea of community has gained a lot of attention in the world and in the church culture. Nevertheless, it is imperative to understand the purpose of community. Community is not about gaining a sense of connectedness or trying to fulfill a void in our lives. The purpose of a church community is to fling others forward into the thrilling, hope-building mission of God in the world. Every disciple of Jesus needs to fling and be flung into hope.

In Revelation 21:25–27, John continues his detailed sketch of the Holy City and notes:

> On no day will its gates ever be shut, for there will be no night there. The glory and honor of the nations will be brought into it. Nothing impure will ever enter it, nor will anyone who does what is shameful or deceitful, but only those whose names are written in the Lamb's book of life.

The ever-open city gates take us deeper into the vision of the church. Most ancient walled cities would shut their gates at night for the same reason most of us lock our doors at night: it was a defensive and protective posture. If a traveler approached the city after the gates were shut, they could try to squeeze their camels and supplies through a small door in the wall (which was referred to as "the eye of the needle"), or they could camp outside the gates and wait until the next day to enter the city.

The open gates of God's Holy City reveal the defenseless posture of the church. Everyone, regardless of race, heritage, social status, or sinful pasts, can be welcomed in at any time. The Holy City does not need to defend itself against any enemies because God really is in control.

Even more, the vision of open gates should remind the church it is a community of people whose arms should always be open wide. The church body exists to see broken people, including those who oppress and persecute the church, enter into God's presence and find healing through the Lamb, who is Jesus.

Surrendered

If we want to live in the Holy City as a fully alive disciple-maker of Jesus, then we must be wholly surrendered and consumed with the ways of God. As the psalmist declared: "My soul is consumed with longing for your laws at all times" (Ps. 119:20).

It is because of our consumed nature that we live with a great concern. We live in the tension of the already-not-yet. We know that God, in Jesus, began a new world—a world where he is King of kings and Lord of lords.

God's kingdom has not been fully restored yet. Darkness, sin, and evil still exist. This is why we must go. We must bring the good news of Jesus. We must be Christ's hands and feet in this world, and we must invite people into God's Holy City.

It should concern us when we see people who might know about God, but they do not know God. It should concern us when we interact with people who do not know God's deep forgiveness. It should concern us when we see evil enveloping the world. It is out of our concern for others that we are mobilized to act.

If your desire is to be consumed with God and concerned for his mission in the world, then there is no better time than now to cry out to God: "Here am I. Send me!" (Isa. 6:8b).

Prayer for Revival

Psalm 119 is known as the longest chapter in the Bible. This psalm is a Hebrew acrostic poem; there are twenty-two stanzas, one for each successive letter of the Hebrew alphabet. It is also a powerful psalm uniquely designed to open up our heart for personal revival. After you close this book, I'd like to encourage you to grab your Bible, find a quiet place, and read through Psalm 119 at a snail's pace. As you meditate, take note of all of the themes we processed throughout this book and ask God to solidify his deep work in your life.

May the Lord be with you. May his face shine upon you. And may you experience a revival of the heart!

Notes

Introduction: The Missing Ingredient

1. Tom Huddleston Jr., "How SpaceX, social media, and the 'worm' helped NASA become cool again," CNBC.com, July 25, 2020, https://www.cnbc.com/2020/07/25/how -did-spacex-and-social-media-help-nasa-become-cool -again.html.

Chapter 1 Ephesus: First and Foremost

1. Craig Keener, *The NIV Application Commentary: Revelation* (Grand Rapids, MI: Zondervan, 2000), 105.
2. Ibid., 106.
3. William Barclay, *The Revelation of John: The Daily Study Bible Series* (Louisville, KY: Westminster Press, 1976), 65.
4. Robert Mulholland, *Revelation: Holy Living in an Unholy World* (Grand Rapids, MI: Francis Asbury Press, 1980), 94.
5. Ibid.

6. Keener, *The NIV Application Commentary: Revelation*, 106.

7. Ibid.

8. Mulholland, *Revelation: Holy Living in an Unholy World*, 96.

9. Keener, *The NIV Application Commentary: Revelation*, 107.

10. Dallas Willard, *The Spirit of the Disciplines: Understanding How God Changes Lives* (San Francisco: Harper Collins Press, 1988), 159–75.

11. Ibid., 175–90.

12. Arsenii Troepolskii, *The Way of the Pilgrim* (San Francisco: Harper Press, 1991), 5–19.

13. Keener, *The NIV Application Commentary: Revelation*, 107.

Chapter 2 Smyrna: Faithful and Fearless

1. Justin Long, "Examining the Real Situation of Martyrdom," John Mark Ministries, March 11, 2020, http://jmm.aaa.net.au/articles/2904.htm.

2. Craig Keener, *The NIV Application Commentary: Revelation* (Grand Rapids, MI: Zondervan, 2000), 114.

3. William Barclay, *The Revelation of John: The Daily Study Bible Series* (Louisville, KY: Westminster Press, 1976), 81.

4. Robert Mulholland, *Revelation: Holy Living in an Unholy World* (Grand Rapids, MI: Francis Asbury Press, 1980), 98.

5. Ibid.

6. Keener, *The NIV Application Commentary: Revelation*, 114.

7. Ibid., 115.

8. Mulholland, *Revelation: Holy Living in an Unholy World*, 98.

9. Ibid., 98–99.

10. Keener, *The NIV Application Commentary: Revelation*, 115.

11. Ibid., 116.

12. Barclay, *The Revelation of John*, 83.

13. John Foxe, *The Voice of the Martyrs* (Alachua, FL: Bridge-Logos, 2007), 3–4.

14. Ibid., 16–19.

15. Ibid., 21–23.

16. Ibid., 51–53.

17. "John Wycliffe," *Christianity Today*, March 1, 2020, https://www.christianitytoday.com/history/people/moversand shakers/john-wycliffe.html.

18. Foxe, *The Voice of the Martyrs*, 240–42.

19. "Nag Hammadi Massacre," Wikipedia, February 3, 2020, https://en.wikipedia.org/wiki/Nag_Hammadi_massacre.

Chapter 3 Pergamum: Loyal and Listening

1. Craig Keener, *The NIV Application Commentary: Revelation* (Grand Rapids, MI: Zondervan, 2000), 122.

2. Ibid., 123.

3. William Barclay, *The Revelation of John: The Daily Study Bible Series* (Louisville, KY: Westminster Press, 1976), 98.

4. Robert Mulholland, *Revelation: Holy Living in an Unholy World* (Grand Rapids, MI: Francis Asbury Press, 1980), 104.

5. Ibid., 105.

6. Keener, *The NIV Application Commentary: Revelation*, 123.

7. Ibid., 124.

8. This is a reference to a well-known quote by Tom Cruise in the film *Jerry Maguire*.

9. Rebecca Lake, "What Is the Average Age of Marriage in the U.S.?" Brides.com, February 3, 2021, https://www.brides.com/what-is-the-average-age-of-marriage-in-the-u-s-4685727.

10. Keener, *The NIV Application Commentary: Revelation*, 124.

11. Mulholland, *Revelation: Holy Living in an Unholy World*, 112.

12. Keener, *The NIV Application Commentary: Revelation*, 126.

13. Ibid.

14. Ibid., 127.

15. Ibid.

Chapter 4 Thyatria: Improving and Intentional

1. Craig Keener, *The NIV Application Commentary: Revelation* (Grand Rapids, MI: Zondervan, 2000), 133.

2. "Ichthys," Wikipedia (accessed January 11, 2021), https://en.wikipedia.org/wiki/Ichthys.

3. In prophetic literature, the imagery of fiery eyes and bronze feet is derived from Daniel 10:6. Frequently, John uses Old Testament imagery to communicate the present dynamics of the New Jerusalem on earth.

4. Robert Mulholland, *Revelation: Holy Living in an Unholy World* (Grand Rapids, MI: Francis Asbury Press, 1980), 113.

5. Keener, *The NIV Application Commentary: Revelation*, 133.

6. Mulholland, *Revelation: Holy Living in an Unholy World*, 118.

7. Keener, *The NIV Application Commentary: Revelation*, 133–34.

Chapter 5 Saris: Alive and Alarmed

1. William Barclay, *The Revelation of John: The Daily Study Bible Series* (Louisville, KY: Westminster Press, 1976), 138.

2. Robert Mulholland, *Revelation: Holy Living in an Unholy World* (Grand Rapids, MI: Francis Asbury Press, 1980), 118.

3. Craig Keener, *The NIV Application Commentary: Revelation* (Grand Rapids, MI: Zondervan, 2000), 144.

4. Ibid.

5. N. T. Wright, *Surprised by Hope: Rethinking Heaven, the Resurrection, and the Mission of the Church* (New York: Harper One Publishing, 2008), 36.

6. Ibid.

7. Ibid., 37.

8. For a broader understanding of the firstborn theology, see the context surrounding Colossians 1:18.

9. Within this section, I am indebted to the scholarship of historian and theologian N. T. Wright. For an exhaustive

treatment of Jesus' resurrection and second coming, see Wright, *Surprised by Hope*.

10. See William Barclay, *The Gospel of Matthew* (Louisville, KY: Westminster Press, 2002), 264–65. The picture of the cornerstone is from Psalm 118:22. Originally, the psalmist meant this as a picture of the nation of Israel. It may be that people reject Christ, and refuse him, and seek to eliminate him, but they will yet find that the Christ whom they rejected is the most important person in the world.

11. Robert Mulholland, *Revelation: Holy Living in an Unholy World* (Grand Rapids, MI: Francis Asbury Press, 1980), 40–41.

12. Ibid.

Chapter 6 Philadelphia:
Persevering and Passionate

1. Robert Mulholland, *Revelation: Holy Living in an Unholy World* (Grand Rapids, MI: Francis Asbury Press, 1980), 124.

2. Craig Keener, *The NIV Application Commentary: Revelation* (Grand Rapids, MI: Zondervan, 2000), 150.

3. Mulholland, *Revelation: Holy Living in an Unholy World*, 125.

4. Keener, *The NIV Application Commentary: Revelation*, 150.

5. The term "Satan" does not necessarily represent a single being—it can mean any adversary of God.

6. William Barclay, *The Revelation of John: The Daily Study Bible Series* (Louisville, KY: Westminster Press, 1976), 147.

7. Mulholland, *Revelation: Holy Living in an Unholy World*, 124.

8. Keener, *The NIV Application Commentary: Revelation*, 152.

9. Ibid.

Chapter 7 Laodicea: Rich and Radical

1. William Barclay, *The Gospel of Matthew* (Louisville, KY: Westminster Press, 1976), 45.

2. Robert Mulholland, *Revelation: Holy Living in an Unholy World* (Grand Rapids, MI: Francis Asbury Press, 1980), 131.

3. Ibid.

4. Craig Keener, *The NIV Application Commentary: Revelation* (Grand Rapids, MI: Zondervan, 2000), 160.

5. Mulholland, *Revelation: Holy Living in an Unholy World*, 131.

6. Keener, *The NIV Application Commentary: Revelation*, 157.

7. Mulholland, *Revelation: Holy Living in an Unholy World*, 132.

8. Keener, *The NIV Application Commentary: Revelation*, 159.

Conclusion: Consumed and Concerned

1. Julia Duin, *Quitting Church: Why the Faithful Are Fleeing and What to Do About It* (Grand Rapids, MI: Baker Books, 2008), 13. Duin sites George Barna's research on the percentage of people who disconnect from the church each year. Duin also notes how Americans are not disinterested in spiritual matters; they are simply not participating in church life to feed a spiritual interest.